Tom Walsh:
Boy Cop, Pilot, Entrepreneur

By Tom Walsh

Copies are available for purchase from Lulu.com

To contact the Walsh family, send an email to mpszut@gmail.com.

ISBN: 978-0-9990538-8-1

Editing and design by Sarah E. White, First Person Productions
Images: from the collection of the Walsh family.

Print
ed in the United States.

Author's Statement

I have tried to tell the truth as far as memory and records have served me. I apologize if I've inadvertently misstated any facts or incidents. No harm is intended.

Contents

Chapter 1: In the Beginning

The integrity I inherited from my mother—to stand up for what I thought was right and take action to honor that, was evident throughout my life from my childhood as well as in my work with the New York City Police Department, in the Navy, and later as a commercial pilot.

An incident from when I was not quite four years old is the first I remember. My father and I happened upon a man arrested by the police. He was lying on the ground on his side with his arms handcuffed behind his back.

An off-duty police officer came by the scene and, upon hearing the crime, became so aroused by the seriousness of the action, that he walked up to the prisoner and kicked him severely in the ribs. Then he stepped back and after listening to further description of the offense, tried to kick the culprit again.

Our parents, Frances Collins and Thomas J. Walsh, date unknown.

I broke loose from my father's hand and tried to restrain the kicking officer by grabbing his pants leg. My father pulled me back and scolded me, but I knew instinctively that it was cruel to kick a disabled man on the ground. Much later in life, I came to defend others in a similar way more than once in the New York City Police Department, NYCPD.

I was the second son of Irish immigrant parents, Thomas J. Walsh and Frances Collins Walsh. I was born at home in Queens on October 19, 1917. I had an older brother, John, born July 15, 1915, and a younger brother, Raymond, born September 16, 1919. He was given the middle name Malachy in memory of our maternal grandfather. Our younger sister, Maura (originally named Rita Mary) was born May 26, 1924, when I was six years old. Another brother was born, christened Lawrence, but he died in early infancy. I don't know the date, but it must have been about 1921.

My father was a taxi driver in New York City. My mother was employed as a nanny to several boys in a very wealthy Manhattan family. Our family lived in Long Island City, New York.

Earning, Learning, Playing

No kindergarten was offered in our school district, so I started school with the first grade at P.S. One, the school just across the street from our home.

When I was maybe 10 or 11 years old, I and my brothers would bring firewood made from the packaging discarded by clothes manufacturing plants to poor neighbor ladies. We were paid by the bushel basket full of firewood, which would earn us about 25 cents—not

Three little sailors: John, Tom, and Ray Walsh, ages about 8, 6, and 4. (Photo taken at our Long Island home.)

quite enough for a pair of shoes, but maybe a couple days' worth of groceries.

I remember one thing that puzzled me: If my older brother was packaging and selling the scrap-wood, he didn't give a fair measure. He would stack it in a loose manner in the bushel basket. But if I were selling it, or my younger brother, we would fill the basket densely. Sadly, John was already beginning to take a troubled path through his life.

We all had our own group of friends; among mine, I was more of a leader than a follower. When our parents were at work, we were pretty much on our own. We had neighborhood baseball teams, put together by the kids. We did not have a regular field to play on but the police had organized a Police Athletic League in which teams from various neighborhoods played and used to keep one block of our street completely free of parked vehicles. I was involved in that. We also played less-organized games, like street hockey on roller skates, using the curbs as the sideboards. When skating backwards, we had to watch out for the manhole covers!

I'm lucky in that my father provided us with high-quality, professional sports equipment. I had a tennis racket suitable for an adult professional. We painted a white line on a flat brick wall and using that as the height of the net, we would serve against the wall.

One of my father's friends worked for Madison Square Garden, a big hockey and basketball arena, and we would attend hockey and basketball games through him.

My boyhood was a happy time for me. I liked to be active, but I also developed an interest in reading, especially historical novels. I'd say I was a patriotic, adventure-seeking, and studious young lad.

When I was 12, in the 6th grade (1929), I submitted an essay to a citywide contest; the required subject was fire prevention. My entry was adjudged the best, and I was awarded a silver medal by the mayor. I suppose it was the completeness of the expression of my thoughts on fire prevention that made it stand out. My studiousness had paid off.

I was aware of the Boy Scouts organization because I subscribed to their magazine, *Boys' Life*. I never belonged to a troop because my dad probably didn't think it was appropriate for us, but I was enthusiastic about the concepts and achievements. On my own I did a number of things that would qualify for merit badges. I made animal traps, wood carvings, and such. I never went camping though.

The values of Scouting appealed to me very much. They guided me to be: "Trustworthy, Loyal, Helpful, Friendly, Courteous, Kind, Obedient, Cheerful, Thrifty, Brave, Clean, and Reverent."

In 1931 I graduated from grammar school, having skipped three terms (a year and a half), and with honors in scholarship. In lieu of a medal, I was given the book

Four siblings about 1930, clockwise from upper left: Tom, John, Ray, Maura.

Adventures in Alaska and Along the Trail by Wendell Endicott.

Mother: Much More Than a Nanny

My mother was born on December 6, 1892 in Turpan, Balinasloe, Roscommon, Ireland.

My mother would speak of her reception at Ellis Island. There, she was told that like all the other immigrants, her paper identification forms were to be attached to her outer clothing. She rejected those instructions, insisting that she was not an animal and could identify herself without paperwork. The official was equally insistent that she attach the forms to her clothing or else she would be the last to be admitted. "So be it," she said. And indeed she was the last, demonstrating certain of her values, among them an innate lack of regard for official red tape, and that she could speak for herself on many occasions.

Recent genetic studies indicate that family DNA traits are conducted from one generation to the next partly via the maternal line. The traits Frances conveyed to her children through genetics come through in many instances in my future activities, as this memoir will reveal.

During my childhood, my mother was employed as a kind of a child's nurse or "nanny" by a wealthy family, where she was one of 32 servants. Her employment connected her with the 400 aristocrats recorded in the annual Social Register. Membership in the elite "400" could be denied to people who were divorced or condemned by loss of the approval of the hierarchy.

Our family was endowed by that relationship with recent copies of the Social Register and copies of Emily Post's volume on good manners. Mother was also given volumes on World War I and the battles in France, which were of interest to us boys. Another benefit: we

Walsh boys inherited her employer's sons' hand-me-down clothes.

My mom came home from work and cooked dinner for everyone. From her employer she had learned the recipes for some of the fine dishes eaten by high society. With my mother's job and witnessing the standards of the wealthy family she worked for, it is only natural that she would bring home their attitudes and disciplines about childrearing. That naturally affected us. How odd to think that a young girl from County Roscommon was teaching us the manners of Manhattan's finest society families!

My mother was a strong disciplinarian who had learned right from wrong in early girlhood from the Catholics and later in the employ of aristocracy. She held high the values of working hard and doing well in school. She was a devoted Catholic and required us to attend Mass and other functions regularly. Infractions of the rules brought on scoldings and physical punishment and deprivation of favorite activities. She expressed her pleasure at exceptional grades in school. She frequently collected garments and sent bundles back to the old country where she had family.

Father: Success in the Taxi Industry

My father was born January 6, 1890 in Culleenboy, Roscommon, Ireland. I don't know any stories from his early years in America, only that he and my mother had not met before coming here.

My father began operating his taxi business at a prosperous time. He was granted the rights to work a taxi line right outside the Plaza Hotel, right across from Central Park in Manhattan. He was able to purchase a second cab, and succeeded as an independent taxi owner. That was threatened in 1927, when the taxi industry was invaded by major companies intent on freezing out the independent operators in a price war. The required taxi emblem was a metal piece in the shape of a shield that would be attached to the right-hand side of the car, right behind the windshield. When my father started in the taxi business, emblems cost $300. Then the big taxi fleets, such as Yellow Cab and Checker, started a rate competition and were able to price the small independent operators out of operation. The required emblem went from $300 to thousands of dollars.

This took place during the Tammany regime, when the Democratic Party political machine rose on the political strength of the Irish immigrant populace. The

Tammany regime was at the height of its power in New York City in the late 1920s.

The stock market crash came in October, 1929 leading to the Great Depression, which worsened over the next years. But even so, my dad was so successful that he purchased more vehicles and opened a limousine service, despite a failing economy.

My mother would describe my father as easygoing; he was modest in his discipline of his children. Nor did he get angry or excited toward her often, although sometimes he expressed his political views pretty strongly. He was a Democrat and committed to control. He was a follower of an early outspoken "rabble rouser" called Father Coughlin, who was radical in criticism of aristocracy and powerful groups in our society. Coughlin's grave fault was expressions of anti-Semitism, which brought his downfall as an opinion leader.

My dad instructed us in mechanical arts. He did his own tune-ups and maintenance on all of his cabs, and made sure we knew how automobile engines worked. He even did the big jobs himself, like changing a transmission.

One day when I was in grade school, I was across the street from the big public school and I encountered a disabled excursion bus nearby with the engine cover open. The driver looked up from his engine and noticed me. He said, "You probably don't know what's involved here." Then he pointed at something and asked, "Do you know what that is?" I said, "That's a carburetor." Then he pointed to something else, and I said, "That's a fuel pump." He went on to ask me to identify various parts of the engine, which I did with complete ease. I'm sure he wondered how I knew!

My dad was cognizant enough of engines that he devised a system for water injection in the fuel supply (which gives an engine a burst of power). Later, when my brother and I were in the service and flying high-powered aircraft, we discovered that Dad's system for injecting water into the engine intake was the same as was used in the military aircraft during dogfights or takeoffs, when high thrust was needed.

Life at home

My parents had a Victrola—a 78-rpm record player—and a large collection of Irish records. The Victrola would be put to use whenever my parents would have friends gather for parties. They would dance to Irish melodies, and we all became familiar with jigs and reels and ballads. Mother had a favorite Irish tenor, John McCormack, and she had records of his songs including "Danny Boy." I enjoyed listening to those records.

My mother enrolled me in violin lessons when I was about 10, and it was quite a distance to the music school. I was given two nickels for the trolley car ride to and from each lesson. I frequently saved the coming-home nickel and instead of riding the trolley, I stopped at Woolworths (often called "the five-and-ten-cent-store") and bought a chunk of milk chocolate that I consumed on the walk home. Those music lessons and a series of lectures in school sponsored by Walter Damrosch on classical music gave us an appreciation for the classics.

In summer, my dad used to take us to the Long Island beaches. We were in the water every weekend, I guess. We learned to swim fairly early, and before long I became a strong swimmer.

My sister Maura (Rita Mary) didn't come along until I was six years old. She was sent away to a boarding school run by nuns in Sag Harbor, over 100 miles away from where we lived in Long Island City. Consequently, I did not see much of her during the school year.

We eagerly anticipated Christmas mornings with thoughts of gifts, and the enjoyment of color and music that accompanied the festival at Church.

Trip to Ireland, 1927

My father did so well in his taxi business that he was able to take our family to Ireland to visit his homeland during the school vacation in the summer of 1927 when I nine years old. We enjoyed a lengthy visit with both sides of our family. Both families lived in County Roscommon and that made for easy visits between maternal and paternal grandparents, and cousins and aunts and uncles, too.

We sailed across the North Atlantic aboard an old German vessel called the Westphalia, and it was a stormy passage. This trip took 10 days; not more than a month or two earlier, Charles Lindberg had flown nonstop from New York to Paris in only 33 hours aloft.

I came back to school the next fall with personal proof that the Earth is round, having seen passing ships rise into view—first the tops of the masts, then the funnels, and finally the bulk of the ships—only to then disappear in reverse order as they drew apart from our ship. Seeing that made me certain of the fact that the earth was not flat.

There was no way at that time to envision my many future crossings of the Atlantic (in hours instead of days), and I recall in grammar school predicting circuits of the earth five times nonstop in less than 24 hours.

Gentleman Tom Remembers…

The following appeared in an article titled "Gentleman Tom Remembers" reported by Clare Kennedy in the Owatonna People's Press, March 15, 2009.

> Walsh can still recall vivid impressions… Their first stop was his mother's home, a cottage with a thatched roof and no central heating, just a fireplace for cooking and warmth.
>
> "I recall that when we arrived at my mother's home there were lots of greetings and hugs and kisses and then mother or someone was pushing me forward to embrace or kiss my grandmother," Walsh said. "And these old Irish ladies had black dresses and black veils over their heads and they looked like something I didn't want to get too close to."
>
> They stayed for two months, which gave young Walsh a chance to experience the slow rhythm of rural Irish life.
>
> "I observed them when they cut turf in the bogs when they cut peat for fires and so forth," Walsh said. "And they had donkeys for pull carts and sheep, lots of sheep."

Charles Lindbergh and Me

I believe that most of the wholesome developments in our lives start with dreams. Mine was to be like Lindbergh—I wanted to fly the Atlantic solo to Paris. In my preteen years, when airplanes were somewhat rare, I would watch any passing plane from the first sighting along its course until it disappeared over the horizon.

I didn't even have a bicycle, but one day I borrowed one and rode to a nearby airport at City of New York—it's not there anymore—to watch the airplanes. They were just tiny, single-engine planes.

I read a book Lindbergh published in 1927, just 47 days after he had completed his historic Atlantic crossing. It was titled *We*, and it was an autobiographical account of his life and the events leading up to that flight.

After that, I would run with arms outspread down hillsides, or lie in the grass in summertime and look up at fleecy cumulous clouds, and wonder how to get there. I was always building balsawood gliders and rubber-band-powered airplanes in the woodshed behind our home. I read all that came to hand about early exploits in the air. I wanted to be the one who "—wheeled and soared and swung high in the sunlit silence where never lark nor even eagle flew—"as John Gillespie Magee, Jr. wrote, in his poem "High Flight."

Tragedy Strikes Close to Me

My first-grade teacher at P.S. One, Miss Renzi, became ill and died late in the term of that then-unmentionable disease, cancer. The school officials collected the whole class together and told us about her passing. At that time, cancer was kept in the dark; it was a scary concept. They called it, "The Big C." That was the first death I was aware of.

The second death was the father of a good friend of mine, named Walter Shea. His dad was a policeman who was shot and killed in the line of duty. I was only 7 or 8 at the time. My friend's mother was designated a police widow and given the job of changing the bedding on the cots in the spare bedroom at a precinct's police station every week.

Walter and I went on to attend the same high school. But also somewhere along the line, he was shot in the eye by a BB gun. It split the pupil in two, which could not be treated. But even with a double pupil in one eye, his vision was good enough and he got into the Air Force later on as a pilot or navigator.

He and I graduated from high school in the same class in 1934. He went on to Syracuse University where he studied Forestry. Seemed like he had a special lead to get into the Air Force at that time. He married a young English woman who was later killed in an air attack in

London. Walter and I drifted apart after high school. I later found a record that he flew in the raids on German oil supplies.

> Officially known as Operation Tidal Wave, the Ploesti Raid occurred on 1 August 1943, and because it marked the second highest loss suffered by the United States Army Air Force (USAAF) in a single operation, it was afterward nicknamed Black Sunday.*

End of Adolescence

In 1932 at the age of 14, I began high school at St. Ann's Academy, an all-boys school. My brother Ray entered the same school two years later. We were both small of build; the boys nicknamed me "Cookie" and Ray was called "the Mouse." We may have been small but we were mighty. I lettered in both Track and Dramatic Club.

In high school I took an interest in theater. In my senior year, a teacher took several of us boys to the professional theater. I saw *Cyrano De Bergerac* three or four times.

In plays produced at St. Anne's, which was an all-boys school, a boy would have to play the women's parts.

* Source: https://www.warhistoryonline.com/instant-articles/black-sunday-ploesti-raid.html

Because I was small I was often cast as the woman. In one play I was seated right behind the footlights, in a dress. At that point I lost any stage fright I might have had. I felt completely relaxed. I crossed my legs at the knee—and that exposed my multi-colored shorts to the audience. They got a big laugh out of that.

My brother Ray and I were exceptional students. In only 10 years we completed the usual 12 years of education, elementary through high school. Both of us excelled in mathematics and science and graduated with honors.

When I graduated from St. Ann's Academy in 1934, I hoped to receive an appointment to the Naval Academy at Annapolis. I had devoted a great deal of my time to reading adventure books and historical novels. I read a history of the U.S. Navy and was enthralled by that. I knew I wanted to be a naval officer.

By coincidence, the same year I graduated, the Tammany regime, which had threatened my father's taxi business in 1927, met its downfall. They were convicted of illegal acts of power and lost the 1934 Mayoral election to the Independent party, whose candidate, Fiorello LaGuardia, was elected. That brought a new power structure to the city.

It seemed that my dad's influence with Tammany may have had a negative effect on my application under

My high school photo and personal statement from our graduation ceremony in 1934.

THOMAS J. WALSH

45-45 21st Street, Long Island City, N. Y.

Track 2, 3, 4. *Literary Endeavors 3.*
Dramatic Club 3, 4. *School Letters 3, 4.*
Class Basketball 3, 4. *Holy Name 1, 2, 3, 4.*

He would make good of bad
And friend of foe.

When a man bites a dog, that's news: when Tom Walsh frowns, that's news. That, in brief, acquaints you with the outstanding trait of this diminutive Senior's delightful character. Not only does his countenance carry a perpetual smile, but his heart is as light as a songbird's, and his spirit as cheerful as the feathered one's spring song.

Cookie's accomplishments do not lie merely in being happy. He has been a star Midget on the Varsity Track team for three years. He was also a member of his class basketball team. But his chief athletic glory comes from his ability as a gymnast. He has also graced the Dramatic Club with his presence for two years. (Remember Elmine?)

Tom aspires to receive an appointment to Annapolis. What is there that could keep a young man with such a spirit as his, from reaching his goal? Anchors aweigh, Admiral Walsh!

the new powers in office; the request for a Congressional nomination required to apply disappeared. I never learned exactly what happened. It was very disappointing to me.

Instead of Annapolis, I began attending City College at night. I still dreamed of flight. But without entrance into the naval training program, how would I somehow reach the sky?

Chapter 2: Keeping the Peace with the NYCPD

From 1937 to 1942—from the time I was 19 until my enlistment in the Navy—I was "the boy cop" of the 9th Precinct of the New York City Police Department on the Lower East Side.

How did I end up entering the police force? I graduated from St. Ann's Academy at age 16, proud that I finished in only three and a half years. The next fall I enrolled in City College, because it was inexpensive and close by. It did not have any campus—all classes were held at night in a local high school. For one semester in 1935, I took courses in math and economics. But then, I got too busy with work. During the day I worked for a bank, and later as a runner/pageboy for the Title Guarantee and Trust company at 176 Broadway, in the financial district of downtown Manhattan. After a year or so of that messenger work, I moved to the real estate division. I would spend afternoons at the County Clerk's office recording documents for the company's files. I became familiar with property descriptions and terminology used in deeds and abstracts. This job laid the foundation for my real estate endeavors later in life.

During this time, my wages were never more than $12 or $15 a week. With the depressed economy of the 1930s and the near future of the banking industry looking dim, my father suggested that I consider training for a well-paying civil service job as a teacher, fireman, or police officer. Civil service jobs paid $60 a week—that was a great wage at that time! I leaned toward police work, maybe because of my experience on the school patrol at P.S. One. While I was in the fifth and sixth grades, I was a crossing guard for children on their way to and from school. I had a special arm band that showed drivers I had the authority to stop traffic in both directions. I would wait until I gathered a group of kids, then stop traffic for them to cross.

In 1937 I followed Dad's advice and enrolled in the Delehanty Institute, a junior college for New York police and fire department candidates. The school offered instruction in both the physical conditioning needed and the criminal procedure aspects of those jobs.

The Delehanty Institute had a gymnastics training facility designed to help you develop yourself to meet the requirements of the police exam. For example, a requirement was weight-lifting: you had to be able to carry an adult body. Another requirement was that you had to be able to scale an 8-foot wall. The wall had no handholds: you just had to run and jump and get over that wall. With continuing practice I managed to do that quite adequately.

When I graduated from St. Ann's Academy, I was just 5 feet 2 inches tall and weighed 110 pounds. A stiff breeze could have carried me off. But while I was in the Delehanty Institute, I not only used their training facility but also made time to work out at the YMCA. It paid off, and I grew in stature and in strength. I achieved 5 feet 8 inches tall, the minimum height accepted by the police force, and I got my weight up to a lean 160 pounds. The Delehanty Institute had made a man of me.

At the end of my Delehanty training I joined some 11,000 applicants taking the police exam; only 4,000 succeeded and made the list eligible for entry. I came in number 461 out of those 4,000.

Nicknamed and Teased as "the Boy Cop"

I want to recognize the transfer of the code of fighting known as Marquess of Queensbury rules to fighting as it was done on the streets of New York. One of the first things I learned after I joined the NYCPD was that, on the street, the Marquess of Queensbury boxing rules I had been taught—no hits below the belt and such—did not apply. Instead, I had to quickly adapt to street fighting techniques where you do whatever you need to do to gain control.

On my first night of duty I was riding in a patrol car as an assistant to an experienced officer. We apprehended a culprit who had demanded access to a toilet in a bar. Upon being denied access, he had smashed a big plate glass window. Then my partner had to take off to catch a hit-and-run driver. He left me with the culprit, saying, "Hold him. I'll be back." He came back shortly after to find me wrestling with this malefactor on the pavement and getting bloodied up from the injuries he had sustained by breaking the window. My partner quickly settled the fighting, scolding me for not using my nightstick right away. The point is the malefactor and I were not fighting with a set of rules. We cops did what was necessary to take control of a situation.

There's an Irish adage that "he who is not the biggest must be the most clever." Given that I was short in stature and slight of build, it is not surprising that I was kidded. As soon as I joined the 9th Precinct, I was immediately nicknamed "the boy cop" and asked what I would do if I met some bad man out there in the streets.

I told them, "Well, we'll see."

Actions speak volumes. I surprised them in my first few months with the number of my felony arrests. These included the arrest of a man with a Browning 45 caliber 1 automatic firearm and the capture of a burglar at gun point in a china shop at 4:00 AM. I also caught a burglar on a fire escape who turned out to be 15-year-old youth, and disarmed a psychologically-disturbed man who had a bayonet.

After these successes, a superior officer confronted those old-timers who teased me by asking, "Why don't you imitate the younger cops instead of looking down at the sidewalk for nickels?" You could say I had the last laugh that time.

The teasing didn't bother me too much because I had years of athletics behind me, including weight training and contact sports. I'd acquired some useful experience and had confidence in my abilities. As a police officer, I was fully ready to serve.

Learning to Be Ready for Anything

I was appointed to jobs in the welfare department and the New York City Tunnel Authority. A number of the Delehanty students hired on the force were Irish-American young men, and we formed a loose-knit group. We called ourselves "the tunnel crowd" because our first job was in the Midtown Tunnel in New York.

Some of the time I worked in the tunnel, responding if there was a traffic stoppage or threat of fire. I spent the rest of my time above ground as a street cop, and I recall many incidents from the 9th precinct on the Lower East side of Manhattan.

The poor—of which there were many in these neighborhoods—relied heavily on the city hospitals for all kinds of medical assistance. When the traditional home remedies didn't work, they'd describe their symptoms to the local pharmacist, addressing him as "Doc," and ask what he might suggest to take care of the problem. In more serious matters of sickness or injury, unable to afford a doctor, they'd call for an ambulance which was then dispatched with a doctor or other skilled aides. The police were usually sent first to certify the need, lend assistance, or record the details of the incident.

At midmorning one day, I was sent to a fourth-floor apartment where neighbors had reported a distraught man threatening others, saying he would jump out of the window. My sergeant had said there was an ambulance on the way. I entered the building by a rear door and met the superintendent who had a master key and directed me to the apartment in question. When I arrived I found the apartment door wide open with a young smiling man standing there barefoot in his underwear. I asked the man his name and he said,

"Louie." Then he said he was going to kill Tony. He appeared incoherent about the reason and rambled on with other unrelated conversation.

The windows were open and I heard the ambulance crew arrive. I walked to the window and waved the crew up. While they climbed the stairs I asked Louie how he would kill Tony. He said, "With my gun in the closet over there." That was just as the young doctor (all dressed in white) came in the door. After a few words from the doctor, Louie agreed to go along with him, and said he'd put on his shirt and pants, pointing out where they were hanging on a doorknob nearby. He picked up the clothing and, smiling, walked back toward me and the doctor. Suddenly he pulled out a bare bayonet that he'd concealed beneath the shirt. Swiftly, he prodded the doctor with the point. I disarmed Louie without too much effort and put him in restraints while he pleaded with the doctor not to hurt him. Needless-to-say the doctor was quite shaken up by then and was thoroughly convinced that Louie needed further attention. He cooperated, and soon we had him dressed and taken away for psychiatric treatment. I locked the apartment.

Detectives returned later to Louie's apartment looking for the gun and other weapons. They found none. The incident was noted in official police records with commendation for prompt and adequate action in the situation.

Knife Fight

Not everything happens on duty. On my way to work a 4:00 PM-to-midnight tour in the 9th Precinct on East 5th Street in Manhattan, I encountered two knife-wielding black men engaged in a fight. I was a few blocks from my destination in a racially and ethnically mixed area of old tenements with street level store fronts, one-way streets lined with numerous working-class bars and small businesses and with cars parked bumper-to-bumper. It was a cool, cloudy afternoon in October, and I was dressed in casual clothes topped by a light jacket that concealed a shoulder holster and my off-duty 32-caliber pistol.

A dozen or so people surrounded the two, mostly white men and a few women. One young woman with a child at her side and a look of anguish on her face was saying to any and all, "Oh, Lordy, make them stop!" Traffic halted in the street, and onlookers watched from upstairs windows. As I came across the scene, there was a break in the encircling group, and I quickly assumed that a barroom argument had spilled out onto the street. The combatants were somewhat inebriated, and, I concluded, neither one was too intent on slaying his opponent.

One of the men was directly in front of me, with his back to me. I jumped into action with a sweeping karate-type kick across the back of his knees. He collapsed in a heap and lost his knife as he hit the pavement. I was over him and had downed and disarmed his surprised adversary before he knew what was happening. I picked up both knives, shook up the fighters, and shoved them off in opposite directions with threats of bodily injury if they went back at it again, using street language they could understand.

A truck driver who saw the 10-second incident remarked, “Wow, has that guy got some balls!” Folding and pocketing the knives, I dusted my hands off on my jacket and continued on my way to work. No names were recorded, no reports or statistics taken; that was just off-duty police work.

Who’s Really Irish?

One day at the main office of the Department of Welfare in downtown Manhattan, I was the officer assigned to keep the peace, intervening in confrontations between caseworkers and relief applicants. Along about late morning, I was called to the reception area to quell a disturbance. I heard the shouting as I hurried to the scene. A young black man, probably in his twenties, was pounding the counter and angrily assailing everyone in sight. Outbursts, both verbal and physical, were not unusual in this locale, but what was most odd was that the man's utterances were in a thick Irish brogue.

As my parents were both born in Ireland, they and their friends had given me a sense of the nuances of Irish behavior, dialect, and mirth, especially when someone was under the influence of drink. I quickly concluded from his appearance and odor that the man was somewhat intoxicated. Catching his attention, I told him he would have to leave and proceeded to escort him to the street. All the while he continued his Irish-accented protest saying, "All I want is me passage home. I've had nuthin' but bad luck, and I curse the day I ever came over here." I told him to shape up, come back when he was sober, and to cut the Blarney. The man stood back, took a long look at me and said, "I'll have ye know that where I'm from we speak the foinest English in the wurruld." "And where is that?" I asked.

"Dooblin, Ireland," he responded proudly. With that, I began to believe him, and more so as he told of his family history going back for generations, their work with the "harses" on landed estates, and his schooling with the nuns. By the time we reached the street, I was convinced that he was really Irish, and wished him well on his next visit to the welfare office.

Time Out to Observe the Character of Some Officers

In the 9th Precinct, on a midnight-to-8-AM tour, I was assigned to a post that adjoined a neighboring precinct. While walking there, I met a cop from that neighboring precinct.

Here's the story he told me.

"Let me tell you about one of your cops. Do see that apartment house in the process of being built? One of your boys had an old black sedan parked where those building materials are stored on the street facing that construction site. I observed him putting several sacks of Portland cement, a keg of nails, and about a dozen 8-foot-long 2x4s into the back of the sedan. It had the back seat removed, making it like a pick-up truck. He also had two 4x8 foot plywood panels stuffed in there. When I came upon him, I asked him what the hell he was doing! He had his uniform jacket and gun belt in the front seat of his car, and he even had a red cloth flag to hang on the back end of the materials sticking out. He replied, 'It's alright, I am a cop,' and he identified himself as being from your precinct. He said he and his brother had a home-building program at his home in Brooklyn and they could readily use these materials in their projects. I told him to get those things out of his vehicle and to get back across the street, or else I would turn him over to my sergeant! He reluctantly unloaded the items and departed."

By this point in my time on the force, it was clear to me that some of my fellow officers had a shortage of the integrity and moral fortitude that the position required. I was doubly glad for my mother's gift of principled DNA and good home training.

There were other officers who would report the issuance of a parking violation ticket in language that read as a heroic venture meriting issuance of medals and ribbons for the dress uniform. And some of the officers received what could either be considered special favors or kind rewards for service above-and-beyond. Take this incident, for example.

On a cool winter's night, an officer named Abe walked side by side with me to adjacent posts for a midnight to 8 AM shift. Abe asked where I would spend my lunch period. I said, "At the all-night open eatery on 14th street." He emphatically objected, saying, "Oh, don't go there! Those drunky bums will fight you, they'll cut the buttons off your uniform and give you a hard time."

I promptly objected, "No, nobody will take buttons off of my uniform, and I can handle any situation that might come up. Where do you go on your meal break?"

He said, "I always find some vacant apartment hallway and sit on the stairs and eat the meal my wife sent along with me." I said, "Abe, you are in the wrong job. You're not ever gonna be happy here." It was just his nature to play it safe.

A couple of weeks later, we were working an 8-to-4 shift as part of a delegation of extra police sent to assist at a parade in midtown Manhattan. That parade ended early in the afternoon, and we returned to our precinct and to our duties. When we got there, ahead of us, four senior day squad police were checking in. ("Senior day squad" means those officers who after thirty years worked daytime only pending retirement.) As the four walked into our precinct they each saluted the lieutenant and said their names and "back from parade duty." With a nod of the head the lieutenant dismissed them, and they went back to the locker rooms and changed into street clothes to go on their way.

I came in behind the last of these and saluted the lieutenant, and he nodded his head too for me to follow the others. Behind me was Abe, the officer I had talked to on that late night shift. He saluted the lieutenant and started to head to the locker room.

The Lieutenant stopped Abe. He said, "Wait a minute!" Then he assigned Abe to a remote post and told him to go. Abe started a protest by saying, "Well, these guys ahead of me had been given the privilege to depart." The lieutenant cut him short and directed him to the distant assignment.

While some might see this as special treatment for individual policemen and wonder about fairness, sometimes appearances are incorrect. Contrary to what others might think, some senior observer might remark that the lieutenant knew something of the nature and performance of difficult assignments and would keep occasions for favors in mind for special distribution when the opportunity arose.

In New York, a Lot Going on Any Time of Day

Around 4:00 AM on a winter morning patrol, I noticed a flashlight-aided search of a desk in a darkened shop across the street. Rapid thoughts flew through my head, such as, if you are opening up early, why not turn on the lights, unless you don't belong there? Moments later, I noticed the shattered plate glass window, which was the point of entry, and so I moved over to where the intruder broke in. Not knowing whether the intruder was armed, I wrapped my hand around the grip of my Smith & Wesson .38 service revolver and commanded the person to come out. His light went out, and he scurried in the dark to the rear of the store.

Just then, a taxi driver dropped off a passenger a block away and slowly rolled by. I told the driver that I needed assistance, and directed him to the police call box another block away. I was assuring myself that the intruder could not find a way out. Then, behind the store, I heard glass breaking. "Oh no," I thought, "he's getting away!" I clattered through the glass of the intruder's original entry point and, shining my flashlight ahead, saw that he had broken through a glass door to an adjacent shop—and noticed me in pursuit. The thief made his exit with a hasty jump through the glass front door of that property. I followed through the same opening. Now I was out on the street, not far behind the man, and commanded him to stop running. He came back toward me. Pointing my gun at him, I quickly got him spread-eagled against the wall. Two armed officers in a patrol car from a neighboring precinct screeched to a stop to assist me.

On the way in to book the prisoner, I asked why the responders weren't from the four cars on patrol in my precinct. The driver said there had been a shooting with police involved at a bar up on the north end. Before I could even start processing my prisoner, the station doors flew open, and a number of police hurried in hauling protesting men before the desk. Within 30 minutes the station was filled with police and city officials and men complaining about the way they were being treated by the officers.

Intoxicated Mother with Small Children

While working on the Bowery one day, I encountered a young woman carrying a baby in one arm and a partially full bottle of wine in the other. Clinging to her skirt was another small child. She didn't appear to have a destination, so I asked where she lived. As she struggled to answer, someone nearby told me her address only a few blocks away. I led her along, making casual conversation, back to her home in an apartment building. Her neighbors stepped out and said they would be sure she was settled in at home.

There was a void between acting "by the book" and knowing how to handle such incidents. She could have been arrested for intoxication and endangerment of minors. But we knew that to arrest such a person would not only be ridiculous, but would also be impractical for taking care of the situation.

A Winter Incident in Harlem

A few minutes before the end of my eight-hour stint, as I walked toward the station house to check in from my assignment, I saw a young woman in the street trying to get the attention of two officers in a patrol car. They either ignored or seemed not to see her, and drove on to the station house. I whistled at her and asked her what she needed.

She replied, "My man, he beat me and throwed me out of the house and I'm 'fraid he kill me if I go back and try to get my clothes and purse."

She was barefoot and wearing only a light sleeveless cotton dress. The temperature at the time was about 15 degrees. I asked if she had any serious injuries or wanted to go to a hospital. Although she was in pain, cold, and scared, she said that she'd go and stay with her girlfriend, if she could only go back to get her things. I said, "OK, I'll help. Where do we go?"

She hurried to an old five-story tenement house and rushed up flights of worn and dirty wooden stairs. I noticed the lath showing through the broken plaster walls as she continued to the top floor, where the trouble always seemed to occur. On the way, she, climbing a couple of steps ahead of me on the stairs, reached down with both hands, grabbed her skirt, and raised it above her waist revealing her bare black thighs and backside. At the same time, she was saying, "Look where he done beat me." I impatiently responded, "Get on with it and continue up the stairs." On the way, she said that she was not married to the man and I told her that I could not make him take her in. She said, "Oh no," and again, "He'd kill me for sure."

Somewhere back in training or through police experience, patrolmen learned that these domestic relationship struggles could be most difficult and dangerous and often included abuse from both parties involved. I had been in police work long enough to know I needed to give thought to what I might encounter on the top floor.

Dressed in my winter uniform of double-breasted blue overcoat with brass buttons, police badge, uniform cap, and insignia, I presented an image of authority, which was generally accepted and respected throughout the city. Beneath the overcoat, I wore two belts; one to hold up my trousers, containing a memo book, billy club, and other personal items; the other a gun belt with a left-handed holster for my .38, spare cartridges, nippers (a restraint tool applied on the wrist) and other items used occasionally. I was also wearing a tight-fitting pair of unlined leather gloves—like hand-wrapping in boxing and providing the same protection.

I was not a big man in any sense and looked very young. And you couldn't tell by looking at me that I was left-handed. This worked to my advantage. As we went up the stairs, I grasped the middle of my nightstick in my right hand. I wrapped its long rawhide thong around my gloved fist.

When the woman and I got to the top floor, she indicated her door and stood off to the side. I rapped with some authority in order to be heard over the partying inside. The door opened suddenly and a big man made a lunge for the young woman while shouting, "…told you I kill you if you bring a cop up here." I shoved him back into the room, telling him with some emphasis to shut up. Then I directed the woman away to the other rooms to get her stuff, closed the door at my back, and surveyed the situation.

There were two other women and three men present and I could see two small boys in bed in another room nearby, asleep in their street clothing. It was my guess that all of the adults were between 20 and 30 years old. There was loud music and drinking in evidence, and the men looked me over with unconcealed disdain. I took measure of them also and read the unspoken suggestion exchanged among them: "We can take him, this'll be easy, just a boy cop on a man's errand, and only a stick in his right hand." The youngest, a slim barefooted male, clad only in a pair of blue jeans, moved catlike out from the group, saying, "I hate cops." He had both fists curled with arms down and out from his sides, and he spat at me as he came within reach.

I reacted with sudden violence. The young male was watching my face. I brought my right hand up with the nightstick. I smashed him across the jaw with the heel of my open left hand. He fell to the floor in a half-seated position, shook his head in disbelief, and took his time getting up. After that, there was a long silence until one of the others in the background softly said, "Man, don't mess with that mother****er; he only slapped him, wooeee."

At that moment, I did not feel too comfortable but followed up with a stern threat, saying, "Anyone else? Now break up the party. Quiet down or else you'll all spend the night in the cooler, understand?" There was no response, but the young woman who brought me there reappeared clad in more than she was wearing when I first encountered her. She was carrying some hastily-stuffed sacks of clothing and personal things and slipped out the door I had opened. With a stern look and a warning twitch of my nightstick, I left, quietly closing the door and following the woman down to the street. She briefly thanked me and hurried off to her friend's house.

I was some 15 minutes late checking in at the police station. A black lieutenant on desk duty for the next shift asked why I had been delayed. He said they were beginning to worry about me. The patrol car team who had ignored the young woman in the street had followed the usual procedure, turning the vehicle over to the midnight-to-eight team on the street at the station house. They had turned in their shift notes to the new command at the desk and then gone up to the locker rooms to change into street clothes. As they came back by the front desk on the way out, he asked if they had seen the young cop from downtown on the way in from their sector. One said that they'd seen me helping some woman, and gave the location.

I told the black lieutenant, without all the details, that I had gone to help a woman in a domestic assault problem and that it had worked out without too much trouble. No need for any paperwork. The lieutenant was a fatherly old cop who knew his neighborhood well. Sensing more than what I told him, he suggested that in the next such incident, I ask for assistance rather than have them find me at the bottom of a stairwell with head broken and weapons gone. I agreed, thanked him for his concern, and departed for home.

It's interesting to note that, after many instances of fighting against officers responding to instances of domestic strife, it was made official policy to send two officers to each request for assistance in a domestic conflict. On too many past occasions, both complaining parties had united to fight the one officer responding.

A Birth Amidst Confusion

During the times of day when school crossings needed to be monitored by police officers, I was assigned a busy intersection in downtown Manhattan that was controlled by stop lights. My job was to stand in the middle of that intersection, wearing white gloves, ensuring motorists understood traffic directions.

On this particular occasion, as the lights turned red and traffic in one direction came to a stop, the lead car continued to roll toward me in violation of the red signal. It was an old sedan with a running board on the side. As the driver came up next to me, he excitedly pointed his thumb toward the back seat where his wife was struggling in advanced stages of baby delivery. He said, "My wife is about have her baby, and we gotta get up to Doctor's Hospital in a hurry!" I grasped hold of the roof, stepped onto the running board beside the driver, and told him to turn his headlights on. I gave him permission to go through red lights, assuring him I would wave the way clear with my white gloves.

With some caution we proceeded through heavy traffic and made it to the hospital. Medics put the troubled woman on a gurney and wheeled her up to the emergency entrance. Well, we were not greeted well by the head nurse! She said we were at the wrong hospital—we should be at Physician's Hospital two blocks away. I protested about the urgency of our visit, but she insisted on her stance that the woman would not be admitted there. It was not what I or the expectant couple wanted to hear, but what could we do? We loaded the woman back into the car and took her to the proper hospital, where she was taken care of.

I was thoroughly annoyed at this dominant senior nurse but followed her orders. On this occasion, my mother's upright DNA stood down. I would have liked to have shown her that, like her, I had a lack of regard for official red tape, but we had no time for an argument with a baby on the way.

1939 World's Fair

Under Fiorella LaGuardia, Robert Moses was named Parks Commissioner and became a great force for change in operations. He proceeded to physically remove the obnoxious Corona garbage dump, which had repeatedly caught fire and could not be extinguished. He had the flaming garbage hauled by barges into Flushing Bay, where it became Riker's Island. The space that was vacated became the site of the World's Fair in May of 1939. I didn't get involved in the fair in any official capacity, but I was glad New York City's leaders were addressing the growing city's problems, such as garbage removal and expansion of the prison system.

War Approaches

That same year, 1939, my oldest brother, John, enlisted in the U.S. Army and was stationed at Schofield Barracks on Oahu in Hawaii. Until then, the three of us brothers had lived at home. I was earning enough to save money, and gave my parents some of my earnings each month for my room and board. The next year my younger brother, Ray, enlisted in the Army Air Corps. He was drafted into the Engineers in December 1941 after the Pearl Harbor attack.

At the start of World War II, I was put in draft status 2B, deferred because police work was considered "necessary for national defense." I was sure I wanted to enlist so I could do flight training. Once the Navy came out with a similar offer, I went to the Draft Board with an argument. I told them it would help the pain of my mother at having her third son go, if they would put me first into 1A classification, but first give me time enough to enlist in the Navy's flight training.

That training program required two years of college, which I didn't have, but the enrollment officers found my good grades from St. Anne's Academy and police service record an acceptable substitute. I was taken into the US Navy V5 pre-flight training program in the summer of 1942.

Learning to fly had been my chief aim since boyhood, and I was finally headed for the sky!

Chapter 3: Join the Navy and See the World

I like to say that most of the wholesome changes in our lives start with dreams. In my preteen years I would watch any passing plane from first sighting until it disappeared; they fascinated me. Now I was about to become a pilot, thanks to the Navy.

The Japanese made a surprise aerial attack on the U.S. naval base at Pearl Harbor on Oahu Island, Hawaii, on December 7, 1941. This air strike climaxed a decade of deteriorating relations with Japan and precipitated the United States' entry into World War II. As a fit young man trained in police work, it was unavoidable that I would become involved.

Government recruiting posters early in the days of World War II invited young men to enlist in the war effort for patriotism and adventure. "Join the Navy and see the world," they promised. To see the world from the pilot's seat sounded appealing to me. My brothers, John and Ray, were already serving the country by this time; in the next chapter I will tell what I know of their service experiences. But first, my "war story."

Join the Navy, See the USA

My deferred draft status allowed me to enlist as an aviation cadet in the Navy V5 flight training program. I began my military service in August, 1942 at Princeton University in New Jersey with ground training and the US Navy pilot training program. I trained in aerodynamics, theory of flight, and meteorology.

I took a special course taught by the flight instructor, Carl Rasmussen. He was chief instructor for a program called Civilian Pilot Training (CPT), hired by the navy to train their pilots. He was my main instructor in actual flight operations.

On my first flight as a student under Rasmussen, he commented on the lack of sensitivity of my feet on the rudder pedals. As I began our takeoff, he stopped me and said, "Take off those clodhoppers." He threw my big boots out the window, requiring me to fly in my stocking feet. Afterwards, I had to go back to the field and find them because they were Navy-issue, and losing them would not have reflected well on this young trainee.

1943: Navy pre-flight training at Princeton. Tom back row, third from left.

The aviation cadets assigned there were housed on the Princeton campus in a facility meant for the rowing crew, located on Lake Carnegie. The lake was artificial, with an island in the middle, and was used for training purposes by the rowing crew. One early morning, I swam out to the island and stepped into the green shrubbery covering it—realizing too late that it was poison ivy. I came down with a severe outbreak of skin lesions and was moved to the University Clinic for treatment—not the brilliant start to my military career I had hoped for!

When released from the clinic, I rejoined my cadet corps and we continued our studies.

Late 1942: Stearman biplane I flew while in the Navy, training at Bunker Hill, Indiana.

Princeton was where we were supposed to train to fly, but the Navy decided they didn't want any flight training within 150 miles of the coast because of possible German U2 submarine surveillance. We cadets were moved to Orwigsburg, Pennsylvania for flight instruction. When that was finished, I was transferred to the University of Georgia, Athens. There, we aviation cadets underwent several months of vigorous physical training in ground studies and active-duty pre-flight.

On Thanksgiving Day (November 26), 1942, I was transferred to Bunker Hill, Indiana for flight training, which took place in Stearman biplane aircraft.

On a solo flight a couple months into that training, while flying over rural Indiana, my engine quit when an oil line broke, spattering oil all over the windshield. I had to make a forced landing and picked the nearest field in sight. I only had about 800 feet of altitude, but I managed to stretch my glide until I was just touching the treetops. I set the plane down safely following the furrows in that small, soft field. Later, when my flight instructor came up with me, I took him out to see the field where I had landed. He tried to make an approach, then said, "I don't know how you did that!" That was my first experience of a forced landing—certainly not the last. When I completed the training, Rasmussen was well enough pleased with the development of my flying talents that, on the day of my flight test for graduation, he just handed me the keys to the airplane and said, "I know how well you fly—go ride around the countryside for an hour and a half."

I received my private pilot's license, but our training was not yet complete.

In early 1943 I was transferred to Saufley Field in the Pensacola Naval Complex in Florida for more flight training. We trained in Vultee BT-13s, before moving on to the Naval Auxiliary Air Station Barin Field on the Florida-Alabama border for advanced training in SN-Js. (The "SN" designation indicates trainer

Early 1943—Saufley Field, after becoming a flight instructor.

aircraft.) In September of that year I earned my Navy pilot wings and was commissioned in the Navy at the rank of Ensign.

Boxing Match

While undergoing training as a Navy cadet at the University of Georgia in Athens, I got called to the center desk to receive a telegram from my father. The cadet officer interrupted my request for the telegram by saying, "Salute me! Salute me, the captain is looking!"

I responded impatiently by saying, "Never mind that crap. Give me the message!" Whereupon a senior Navy officer observing interceded, and he saw that I got the message. Then, he added that he wanted me and the cadet officer to fight each other in the boxing ring on the next occasion. The cadet officer was probably two or three inches taller than me and outweighed me by perhaps 15 pounds. But, I accepted the commitment. With several years of police work and boxing and fighting in my recent experience, once in the ring I made this cadet officer look timid and not up to the standard of fight expected. After one round, the officer (who turned out to be trainer for the world champion boxer, Jack Dempsey) closed the encounter without any further comment. This displayed the inherited aggressiveness which I brought into my Navy life.

I Became a Flight Instructor

I had the option of continuing training to become a carrier-based fighter pilot, but was retained at Pensacola as a flight instructor. As I shifted from student to teacher, I observed that flight instructors do not so much teach flying, as lead beginners in the coordination of

Navy service portraits. I earned my pilot's wings in September, 1943.

WALSH

T. J. WALSH
USNR

hand, mind, and machine to safely achieve the mastery of flight.

After many months and hours of experience I was promoted to Lieutenant Junior Grade and was ordered to Navy Operational Training at Naval Air Station Sanford near Orlando. Our training flights mostly occurred over the Atlantic Ocean to the east.

During this period I became involved in an anti-submarine mission as a crew member on a Patrol Bomber Y (US Navy medium-to-heavy, twin-engine amphibious aircraft used for maritime patrol, as a water bomber, and for search and rescue). We flew a 15-hour night flight in the Gulf of Mexico proceeding from Galveston, Texas all the way down to the Florida Keys. I flew with primitive radar aboard over convoys en route from New Orleans, Louisiana to Key West, Florida, and in the Gulf of Mexico, and also made "no lights" surveillance flights in the Pensacola, Florida area.

The Dilbert Dunker

My role in the Navy operations at Sanford required that I take part in new equipment trials. One piece of equipment was the Dilbert Dunker, a crash simulator used to train pilots in escaping airplanes forced to crash-land in water. (The name is a reference to a World War II-era cartoon character in Navy aviation training videos and posters who was incapable of doing anything right.)

The Dilbert Dunker mimicked the design of a single-engine propeller airplane. The idea was to simulate a crash in the sea where the plane would briefly be above the waves, then the weight of the engine forward would cause the rest of the airplane to sink with it, upside down. The Navy facility had a set-up where a damaged airplane (no longer able to fly) would slide down a chute to simulate an aircraft landing in the water.

The cockpit, with canopy retracted, would rapidly fill with water. Each pilot we trained was taught to get out of his shoulder and parachute harness, swim out of the airplane, and try to swim to the surface. In the test facility, two divers went underwater with the sinking aircraft; they were equipped to cut the pilot loose from the shoulder harness or any other restrictions to his efforts to leave the airplane. Since the plane was at that point sinking upside down, the pilot had to swim down to get out of the cockpit, then to the side and up to the surface. The divers were there to assist or to remove the pilot in any way necessary.

As a pilot, I trained in the Dilbert Dunker and had to execute my underwater escape. I actually did it. Once up on the dock, reviewing my action with the supervising officer, he remarked that I had blood on the arch of one foot. Apparently I had exited the cockpit a bit too soon as it went down the "Dunker" slide, and kicked the top of the windshield, injuring my foot.

I didn't fear the Dunker since swimming came easily to me, because my dad had taken our family to beaches near New York City. I was glad now that I had that early experience swimming in the ocean surf.

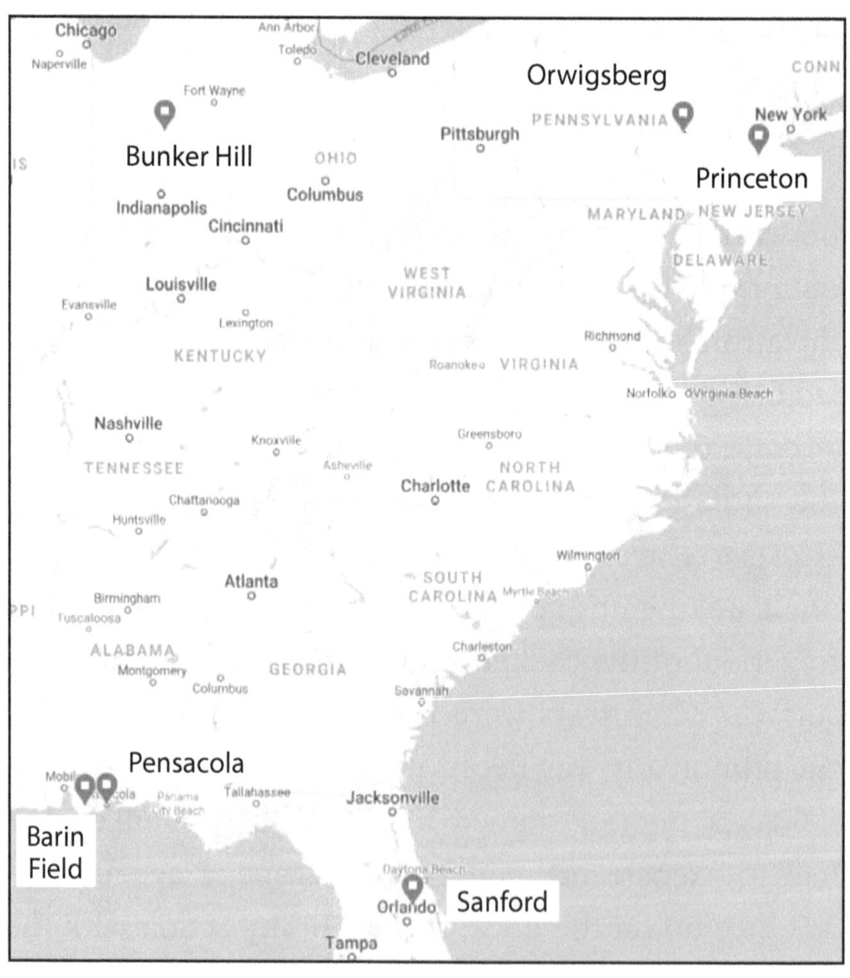

High Flight, by John Gillespie Magee

Oh! I have slipped the surly bonds of earth
And danced the skies on laughter-silvered wings:
Sunward I have climbed, and joined the tumbling mirth
Of sun-split clouds—and done a hundred things
You have not dreamed of—wheeled and soared and swung
High in the sunlit silence. Hov'ring there,
I've chased the shouting wind along, and flung
My eager craft through footless halls of air.

Up, up the long, delirious, burning blue
I've topped the wind-swept heights with easy grace
Where never lark, or even eagle flew—
And, while with silent lifting mind I've trod
The high untrespassed sanctity of space,
Put out my hand and touched the face of God.

According to *Air Force Magazine,* Pilot Officer John Gillespie Magee Jr., the author of "High Flight," the best-known poem about aviation, was killed on Dec. 11, 1941, when his Supermarine Spitfire collided with another airplane over Britain. He was only 19 years old. An American serving with the Royal Canadian Air Force, Magee had written "High Flight" in August or September and mailed a copy to his parents in Washington, D.C.
[source: https://www.airforcemag.com/chronology-1940-1949/]

In Service to Women

At the end of my first week of training at Pensacola, I was waiting for the last bus scheduled for an 11pm departure from town back to base. I was on board the bus with two enlisted men waiting for a driver and other passengers. Finally the driver came out to the bus, opened the door, retrieved some paperwork from driver's area, then exited and closed the door on 20 enlisted Waves (women Navy Reserve members) who were waiting to board.

It had started raining, and he shouted at the young women to get back and form a line two by two. Then the driver went back into a neighboring tavern, leaving the Navy personnel out in the rain. By then, we were 20 minutes behind the scheduled departure. I got up from my seat in the bus, went to the front, opened the door, and told the women to climb aboard. I then went to look for the driver and found him inside the tavern, chatting up a waitress at the end of the bar. I got his attention and told him he was behind schedule and some of the passengers were due to their home bases by midnight. I asked his name, which he would not divulge. I told him that it wasn't needed as the bus could be identified. He protested in strong language, saying that he didn't take orders from me and was not in the "bleep, bleep Navy" and he would go on his own time.

I went back aboard the bus, and the driver came out. We proceeded to our destinations; Bronson and Barin Field. Barin Field was out on the Florida/Alabama border some 35 miles from Pensacola. We arrived there half an hour late for some of the people aboard, and I put together a formal complaint to the officer of the day (OD). The OD was not available at that time, and I had hoped to handle it the next day, but was still unable to file the complaint the next day.

I was reassigned to training in Pensacola and left on the last bus of the day, at almost midnight, for another high-altitude training. There were only two enlisted men on the bus and the bus driver turned out to be the same one as the week before. We were on the road in an undeveloped area when the driver stopped the bus, got out of his seat, and said, "Hey, wise guy, why don't we get off here and discuss our earlier disagreement?" It was obvious he wanted to abandon me on the roadside. I was careful not to get between him and the door. In an effort to push me out, he swung at me and knocked my hat off. My reaction was immediate, and with several years of police and combat training, I drove him back into his seat and told him the next stop was going to be the Shore Patrol in Pensacola.

After that, we proceeded on our journey. I asked the two enlisted men to comment on what happened.

One said he was going to a funeral and the other man said he wasn't aware of anything that had happened. We made our statements at the Shore Patrol Station and departed on our separate ways.

Several days later, the Admiral declared that he was tired of these drunken young officers causing trouble and making criticisms. I was called to my Captain's office and told that I was under house arrest, what we called "in hack," or confined to quarters except for meals and my flight duties pending a hearing before the Admiral. A couple of days later, a young lieutenant lawyer from New Hampshire called on me and said he would represent me in the hearing before the actual court martial. He documented my story, which included the bad language used by the bus driver and other statements made that were not to the driver's credit. He got all of the details that I had not been able to put forth earlier.

I was at my duties on the tarmac that day when my Captain and attorney returned from the hearing before the Admiral. The Captain returned my salute as he got down from his airplane and then embraced me, saying that I was released from my condition "in hack." The Admiral was well convinced that I was in the right in what I had done. He wished he had more upstanding young officers in his command.

(After I was released from naval service in 1946, I had a chance to visit The Navy Department in Washington DC and had an opportunity to view my service record. I learned that my finest fitness report was from that period of my time in the Navy. The bus driver picked the wrong little Irish guy to start a fight with that night.)

French and English Flight Students

During World War II, the U.S. Navy had an agreement to work with our allies in training pilots. As flight instructors at the base in Pensacola, we had French and British flight students, and we had a few problems with them.

The French pilots were somewhat experienced, and it was mostly a matter of becoming used to our aircraft before returning to France. One day, walking on the base, I observed a French uniformed officer who ranked several grades above me. As I saluted him I said "*Bon matin, Monsieur,*" French for "Good morning, sir" that I'd learned at St. Ann's Academy.

He stopped and asked my name and where I was assigned. He said, "I want you as one of the instructors of the French pilots coming here."

I said, "No, My French is not good. It just wouldn't do."

He said, "It will work out."

Then I became a flight instructor, and it was mostly flying at night. With just a few commands I was able to fill that job. One important moment was when I handed off the airplane's dual controls to the copilot, and I learned to say, "I've got it" and "You've got it."

We got through that program without any mishaps.

We also had aspiring English RAF pilots, and one day on a test flight I directed a young man to put us into a tailspin to the left and then recover. He proceeded to climb up beyond the point of having any control of the flight, and the plane stalled. Then, it kicked off into a spin. Well, on such tests one would let the airplane spin perhaps two circuits and then recover. But this man failed to do anything to bring the aircraft out of the spin. I said to him several times to recover, recover! All he did was hold the stick tighter and pull it back into a stalled position. After several attempts to get him to release the stick—and of course we were losing altitude at a rapid rate—I used some basic cuss words to tell him that he gotta let go! Then I was able to get the stick into a neutral position, and stop the spin and recover. Afterwards, in the review on the ground, I asked what finally got him to release the controls. He said, "Why, you used such atrocious language, sir, it caused me to relax."

Hotshot Flyers

At the time of the Normandy invasion I was about to finish my stint at Pensacola as an advanced flight instructor when an incident occurred that I thought would have me dressed down in rank, if not ejected from the Navy. I was lead pilot in a flight that day consisting of a formation of six advanced trainers on a gunnery mission. Air traffic at Barin Field, where we were to land, was extremely heavy.

As a flying instructor, I had established an elaborate procedure for the break-up of formations and the proper spacing of aircraft. On heading away from the field (twelve miles back), several thousand feet above the pylons at "Point Able," as the lead pilot I gave the signal to break. The first in the echelon did a wing over left diving turn, down toward and between the pylons. Meanwhile I remained at an altitude above the formation, slowing my speed so I would arrive at an altitude of 800 feet above field elevation, with proper interval behind any other aircraft ahead of me in the slot.

As the instructor, I was the chase pilot flying behind and above the formation, observing techniques and making notes on my kneepad. I proudly noted that my flight broke up with precision, and I followed tightly behind the last man. When I was almost abeam of the left pylon there came a swift intruder at overtaking

World War II aircraft of the types I trained pilots to fly. Sources: thedrive.com, ww2aircraft.com, thanlont.blogspot.com.

speed and in violation of the Navy's sternly fixed procedure when he put his wing in ahead of me and turned to grin at me. With the plane canopy closed and as he was wearing a flight helmet and goggles, he looked like scores of other pilots who might be aloft at that time.

I assumed that he was some hotshot kid showing off and breaking strict rules, entering the restricted, very dense approach pattern. I flew up, in close, and tried to wave him back out of his slot. I dipped my wing and skidded aggressively toward him, but to no avail. He and I maneuvered for advantage all the way to a side-by-side landing on the base runway. On the taxiway, the mystery pilot raised his goggles and removed his helmet, and then I recognized the pilot as my squadron commander!

It was about noon the same day, and I was wondering if I would be called to account soon, but no message arrived at lunch, nor after the afternoon flights. On my next evening visit to the Officer's Club, I noticed a senior pilot who was just back from a second tour of combat duty. He outranked me by several grades. With a smile on his face, he said that on his next assignment with the fleet he'd like to have me on his team. "For a little guy," he added, "you are surely aggressive." I was completely surprised by the pilot's lack of criticism of my tactics. I attempted to tell him my initial assumption—that he was some brassy pilot—but then, recognizing his skill, I had picked up the challenge and "fought" him all the way to "touchdown." I also told the senior pilot that I attributed my aggressiveness to my police experience before enlisting. "At the start of an encounter it was crucial to quickly determine the desired outcome and decide what actions to take to achieve that goal with precision and grace," I told him. It had held true on the streets of New York, and it held true now in the cockpit.

Religious Freedom

Similarly, I found it necessary to stand up for my religious freedom. For my first few Sundays in the Navy, I was required to attend a non-denominational religious service, which I found contemptible because I was denied the right to attend a Catholic Mass. On a particular morning, I was seated in a prominent spot in the front row of the balcony, and I refused to stand or kneel or participate in the proceedings. Afterwards, I was taken aside by the commanding officer and criticized for my disrespectful attitude. I stated to him that within the past week or so President Roosevelt and Winston Churchill had met in the North Atlantic and proclaimed warfare on behalf of the Four Freedoms, one of which was Freedom of Religion. The CO said I would be better regarded if I displayed more respect in the future. I did learn several stanzas of the Navy Hymn and would join in on various occasions with great fervor and enthusiasm, mellowing in the process.

More Training at Naval Air Station, Glenview, Illinois

After being promoted to Lieutenant Junor Grade, I went to the Naval Air Station (NAS) in Glenview, Illinois for training in carrier landings aboard the USS Wolverine on Lake Michigan. I completed eight carrier takeoffs and landings and one catapult shot on August 10, 1945. I was the lone pilot picked for catapult takeoff (which for training purposes took place from a stationary platform rather than from a moving aircraft carrier). That was quite a thrill. The instructions were emphatic: Hold your arm up when the engine was running at full power, but restrained by the catapult's bridle. When you were ready, you retracted your arm to signal the crew to release that restraint. You had to expect your body to be pulled backward by the force of acceleration—there was a cushion behind the pilot's head to mitigate the G force.

When I was catapult- and carrier-qualified, I was assigned to crew operational 15-hour anti-submarine patrol flights in PBYs (patrol bombers). I took part in new equipment trials. On the one occasion I catapulted in a Navy F6F Hellcat and qualified in carrier landings and take-offs on the USS Sable. I flew Stearmans, Vultees, SNVs, North American Texan SNJs, PBYs, Grumman F6F Hellcat and FM2s. With all of this experience, I was being considered as a test pilot.

An Unconscious Flyer

There was a story some years ago about a pilot named Payne Stewart, a professional golfer, who fell unconscious while flying his personal Lear jet. Others on board could not rouse him and the plane kept on flying until it ran out of fuel and crashed in a remote area. I had a similar experience when I was flying for the Navy in Glenview, Illinois. They sent us up in pairs of planes, one pilot each, for high-altitude testing. We were on voice restriction but we had lots of signal strength. The pilot next to me stopped communicating—he just cruised along, not doing anything. I flew close and waved at him but couldn't get any response. So, I took it upon myself to wake him up. I maneuvered my plane's wing tip next to his, got my wing up under his, and gave it a small jolt upward. He looked up in surprise, got on his oxygen mask, and recovered. We landed safely. I'm glad he didn't meet the golfer's fate.

Transition Back to Peacetime

After my training at the Naval Air Station in Illinois was complete, I received orders to Pacific Fleet duty, joining the Carrier Aircraft Service Unit 66 at San Diego, California. During this shakedown period I was on track to join a Navy combat team that would join a flying squadron's operations in Japan. Then on August 6, 1945, the United States detonated nuclear weapons over the Japanese cities of Hiroshima and Nagasaki. Shortly after, the Japanese surrendered. Instead of deploying, I was assigned as a pilot to bring some war-weary planes from Seattle to storage facilities in Oklahoma and Arizona.

While waiting for discharge, I took Nuclear Physics at the Naval Institute, studying the development of the atom bomb. The information in the course was classified and secret. I successfully completed the course with a grade of 4.0 and earned a promotion for pending rank of Lieutenant Senior Grade.

I was discharged from the Navy in New York on January 8, 1946. Had I chosen to stay in the service, I might have qualified for test pilot status. Given my flying skills and the cooperative attitude that had led to my testing and new training and flying techniques, like catapulting and water rescues (thanks to the Dilbert Dunker), I might well have been headed for a career as a Navy test pilot.

Instead, I followed a plan a friend and I had made while serving in Pensacola together. Glenn Degner and I set out to bring an airport to his home town of Owatonna, Minnesota.

1946: Bringing an Airport to Owatonna

Glenn Degner was my roommate in Bachelor Officers Quarters (BOQ) at Saufley Field, where he was staying pending his wife's arrival. Glenn recognized the need for a good regional airport in his hometown of Owatonna, Minnesota. His work assignment at Saufley Field was Safety Officer, and I flew with him through several practices during our flight training. He was sufficiently impressed with my flight skills and he proposed that at the end of our service, we proceed to Owatonna to establish a regional airport. He thought our fellow serviceman, Joe Dulak, an airplane mechanic, would also make a good partner in the enterprise. After due consideration, I agreed to join Glenn and Joe in planning an airport. But first, we each had to finish our respective commitments to the Navy.

Joe Dulak made the acquaintance of Ted Williams, the world famous professional baseball player who before joining the Navy had played for the Boston Red Sox. By the end of Joe's military service, the two had established a great friendship. Ted Williams would become a strong supporter of our efforts to establish an airport and an important part of our public relations efforts.

Upon discharge from the Navy, I kept my promise to Glenn to join him in the aviation business. We set out from New York where we had been discharged and drove to Washington D.C. to pick up Glenn's wife, Billie. We stayed overnight in a motel and, while we were in the area, made contact with Ercoupe, Maryland-based manufacturers of a low-wing monoplane.

The next morning, we were about to depart on our cross country tour, when we discovered a man had broken into our car. As we approached on the passenger side, we saw him sitting on that side, wearing one of Glenn Degner's jackets. When what he was doing became apparent, I ran around the car to the driver's side and called back to Glenn to call the police. The intruder had moved over and tried to come out on the driver's side, and I restrained him from leaving the car. The police finally arrived and took him to court to charge him. We did not want to be delayed with charges and procedures in court. So, we just let it go, and proceeded on our journey.

The three of us then drove across country to Owatonna, Minnesota. As we drove, we stopped at several aircraft companies, such as Piper in Pennsylvania and Aeronca in Ohio. If we were going to start an

8/28/46 Cashman Field: R.W. Kaplan and T. Walsh depart for Chicago, Pittsburg, Washington, New York, and many other stops enroute with plans to return to Owatonna, MN 9/4/46.

aviation business, we needed to have a stock of airplanes, both to fly and to sell to other pilots.

On arrival in Owatonna, we negotiated with members of the Cashman family to lease land on West Bridge Street for a temporary airport until a permanent location could be developed. At the same time, the Owatonna Municipal Council purchased farmland on which to build the permanent airport.

On April 28, 1946 the Owatonna Regional Airport opened at Cashman's Field while the new site was under construction. The opening-day festivities drew a crowd of approximately 500 people. As President and Chief Pilot of Southern Minnesota Aviation Service (with Glenn Degner, Joe Dulak, Bob Crocker, Terry

Tom Walsh of Southern MN Aviation Service at the temporary airport in Owatonna, MN.

Cashman, et al), I was the first to take off from the airport, flying a Piper Cub. We were officially open for business. Southern Minnesota Aviation Service (SOMINA for short) engaged in a flight training operation for WWII veterans, as well as charter flights, and local recreational flying. We introduced our customers to corporate flying activity to enhance their production and product distribution and sold four Ercoupe airplanes to local companies. Ted Williams visited the Owatonna Airport after his release from service as part of a public relations event. I recall watching him mugging for the cameras, swinging a bat in the office of

From left: Joe Dulak, Glen Degner, Tom Walsh. Southern MN Aviation Service, Inc. received this official plaque commemorating the airport's founding, 1946.

our new enterprise there—much too close to a big plate glass window. I worried but fortunately no harm was done. Photos of Ted Williams were displayed in the airport—probably some taken that day.

I'd met Ted Williams in the Navy myself, while serving as Squadron Duty Officer in Pensacola. I had an enlisted yeoman working with me. We had to close down the area where we had done flight instruction for cadets. Some enlisted men were standing around. The commanding officer stuck his head out of his office door and said, "Lieutenant—give those guys a job.

Have them sweep down the deck. Then send them back to quarters, because they're only going to make mischief around here." I grabbed a number of push brooms with the yeoman and approached the group. All but one slipped away. The last fellow turned around, and I presented him with the brooms and I said, "Get your friends and sweep down the deck in this area, then get back to quarters." When I got back to my workplace, I said to the yeoman, "I understand that Ted Williams is a student here. Point him out to me if you see him." He said, "That was Williams you gave the brooms to."

From April 28 to September 3, 1946 I was directly involved as Southern Minnesota Aviation Service engaged in fixed base operation at Owatonna's first primitive airport. I flew chartered trips, helped with aircraft sales, and gave flight instruction. I soloed R.W. "Buzz" Kaplan on May 18, 1946 in a Piper J3 Cub airplane from our primitive grass strip airport in Owatonna. He was a young man just home from military service like me. It was my observation many years ago that flight instructors do not so much teach flying but more likely lead beginners in the coordination of hand, mind, and machine to safely achieve the mastery of flight. Over the years since, I've observed Buzz improve on these skills and extend his influence on aviation to the benefit of our country and the world at large.

Buzz became an aviation legend in Owatonna and was eventually inducted into the Minnesota Aviation Hall of Fame. My last adventure with SOMINA was a trip I flew with Kaplan in his Ercoupe to New York and back, with many stops en route.

During my time with SOMINA I met the Wesely girls and courted Martha, whom I married in 1947. In three action-packed years I had gone from a young man dreaming of flight to a Navy veteran, a seasoned pilot, and next, an aviation entrepreneur—and not yet 30 years old!

I left Owatonna in late spring of 1947 to return to the New York City Police Department (NYCPD), where veterans' preference rights were still valid.

Martha on our honeymoon in Niagra Falls, Canada, 1947.

Chapter 4: My Brothers in Arms

In the last chapter I relayed my experiences during my military service. Now I turn to the experiences of my two brothers, John and Raymond.

Raymond, Thomas and John Walsh, 1946

John Joseph Peter Walsh, US Army Artist

In 1939 my older brother, John, enlisted in the US Army and was stationed at Schofield Barracks on Oahu in Hawaii. In 1942, shortly after the Pearl Harbor attack, his unit was moved to the South Pacific at Guadalcanal.

From Guadalcanal, his unit proceeded across the Pacific to New Guinea and other islands in the Indonesian archipelago. He was put to work making maps showing enemy positions, as far as they were known. From then on I don't recall much, as he was not good about communicating with family.

John's life was never smooth, and we were not close. It ended in 1961 when, on July 15th, my brother's body was found in New York City's East River.

Raymond Malachy Walsh, US Army Air Corps

In 1940 my younger brother, Ray, who had finished two years at St. Peter's College in Jersey City, New Jersey, and gone to work for an insurance company in lower Manhattan, volunteered for the pilot program of the Army Air Corps. He was accepted as a cadet. But, while he waited for his first assignment, he was drafted into the Army Engineers. (The US had instituted the first peacetime draft that year.)

Ray completed basic training at Fort Leonard Wood in Missouri. He was almost sent to the Philippines with the Army Engineers but luck was with him. He was plucked out of that outfit for flight training in the Air Corps. That was fortunate because, otherwise, he would have been among the troops stationed in the Philippines who were later captured on the Bataan Peninsula and forced into what became known as the Bataan Death March. Many atrocities were committed by the Japanese guards, and hundreds of American soldiers died.

Instead, Ray received pilot training in Texas. When he got his wings, he was made a Staff Sergeant, but not enrolled as a 2nd Lieutenant (the lowest officer rank) as his companions were. He continued his service status while the rest of his troop became commissioned officers. At some point he complained to my father, who took it upon himself to communicate with the Secretary of War. Ray was called one day by his commanding officer and instructed to get himself some uniforms: he was about to be commissioned. Ray and I kept in touch by exchanging letters during the war, so I know something of his military exploits.

The Making of a Flying Ace

Ray caught up with his companions from pilot training, and they were sent in April, 1944, to England to fly in the 9th Air Force. He was just 24 years old. Their job: to fly combat missions against the Germans over France. Ray was part of the 406th Fighter Group, which entered combat in May as the Allies were preparing for the Normandy invasion. They flew P-47 Thunderbolt aircraft, with which I was familiar from my work as a flight instructor back in the US.

Evolution of Military Aviation

On June 20, 1941, just days after the Normandy Invasion, the Army Air Corps became the United States Army Air Forces (USAAF), giving it greater autonomy from the Army's middle-level command structure. Until 1947, the responsibility for military aviation had been divided between the Army for land-based operations and the Navy and Marine Corps for sea-based operations from aircraft carriers and amphibious aircraft. The United States Air Force became a separate military service on September 18, 1947 when The National Security Act of 1947 created the National Military Establishment, later renamed the United States Department of Defense, which was composed of four of the five branches: the Army, Marine Corps, Navy, and a newly created Air Force.
[Source: https://en.wikipedia.org/wiki/History_of_the_United_States_Air_Force

According to Nomad Mobile Guides' page on the 406th Fighter Group, they "…provided area cover during the landings in June, and afterwards flew armed-reconnaissance and dive-bombing missions against the enemy, attacking such targets as motor transports, gun emplacements, ammunition dumps, rail lines, marshalling yards, and bridges during the campaign in Normandy."*

Ray had written lengthy letters to me during that time in response to my complaints about our US combat aircraft being slower than the enemy's and failing to perform as promised in the aircraft publications. Perhaps it was Churchill who said, "We'll do the best we can with the tools we've got." Our Navy dictum for fighter pilots was, "the best defense is a strong offense." Brother Ray filled his letters with detailed sketches of some of the outnumbered combat actions he had survived.

The first of those actions earned him a Distinguished Flying Cross, a promotion to Captain, and considerable media attention. The story has been told several ways in several sources, so I rely on my memory of what Ray wrote to me in his letters.

* Source: http://abmc.nomadmobileguides.com/Normandy.php?page=narrative&id=cont-2988

The Normandy Invasion began on June 6, 1944. On June 11, Ray became the first American to shoot down a German "doodlebug"—an unmanned bomber also called a "buzz bomb" but technically, a V-1 flying bomb. (In German, the term was Vergeltungswaffe, which translates as "Vengeance Weapon.")

It was late in the afternoon, and he was aloft at considerable altitude, heading back to base in England from a flight to a US airstrip in France, when he saw what looked like a German fighter plane—all black, swastikas on the side. He turned altitude into speed by descending and caught up with the plane. When he got close, he discovered that there was no pilot—just a plane full of bombs, clearly destined for London. Ray shot the wing off. The doodlebug plunged into the English Channel and exploded on impact. He received his promotion to Captain two days later and was awarded the Distinguished Flying Cross in recognition that he probably saved many lives with his bravery.

This sensational incident was reported back home in New York in the Daily News on June 20, 1944. A comic-book style depiction appeared in print as well (but in what newspaper is lost to history).

At that time, Coca-Cola sponsored an international radio program called "Heroes All" that broadcast from London. I was newly enrolled as an aviation cadet in

The comics publishing industry was in its infancy when World War II began: The US Army borrowed their graphic style to unite people behind the war effort in publications like the Stars and Stripes.

the Navy's V5 program stationed at Saufley Field near Pensacola, Florida. My father sent a telegram to alert me about the radio program. The Officers' Club had the best radio on the base, so I went there to tune in the station.

I was a very junior officer—when I asked the officers to pipe down, they didn't pay any attention. But then the commanding officer overheard me and said, "What's the trouble there, son?"

I replied, "I'm trying to hear my brother from England."

He said, "pipe down" and got the rest of the officers to quiet down.

We listened to Ray being interviewed on the radio program. He described how he came upon what he thought was a German fighter plane, shot the wing off it, and saw it do a slow roll before diving into the English Channel.

Other Triumphs

On June 23, flying over the French countryside, Ray destroyed a German ammunition truck. A spectacular photograph of that moment, captured by his wingman's gun, was printed in a newspaper, but again, which newspaper is unknown.

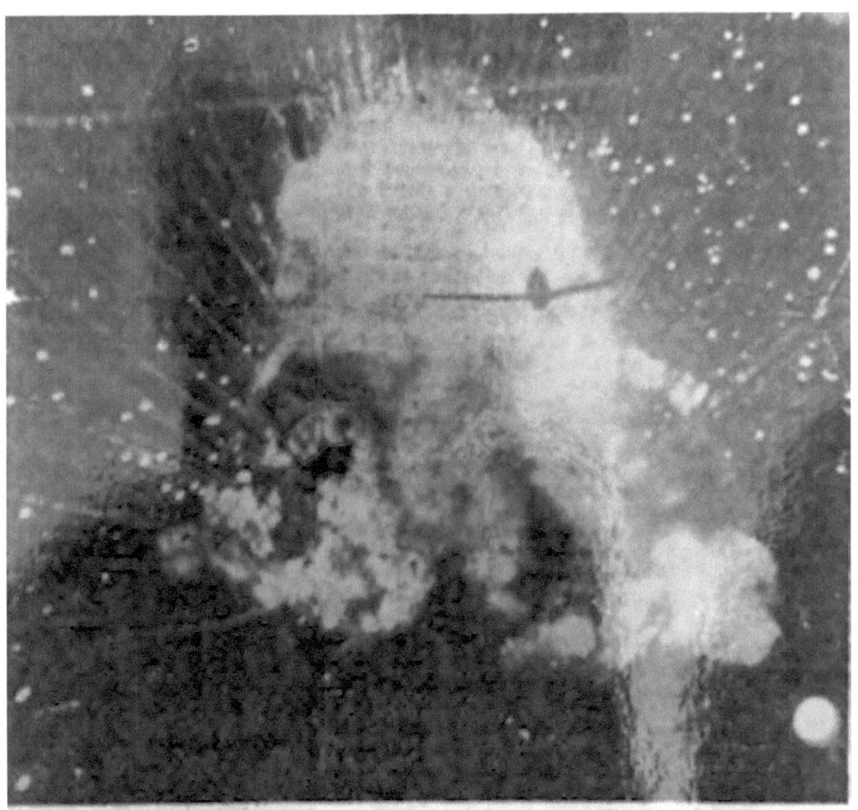

Riding spectacularly, but safely, out of the chaos of destruction it has just achieved, a P-47 Thunderbolt is seen framed in this remarkable action picture. Pilot Capt. Raymond Walsh, Long Island City, N . Y., had risked his neck flying low to blast a German truck carrying ammunition to the Breton front, and is seen virtually engulfed by flame while the plane comes bravely through.

Newspaper photo caption: Riding spectacularly, but safely, out of the chaos of destruction it has just achieved, a P-47 Thunderbolt is seen framed in this remarkable action picture. Pilot Capt. Raymond Walsh, Long Island City, N.Y., had risked his neck flying low to blast a German truck carrying ammunition to the Breton front, and is seen virtually engulfed by flame while the plane comes bravely through.

"La Belle France" dated September 26, 1944

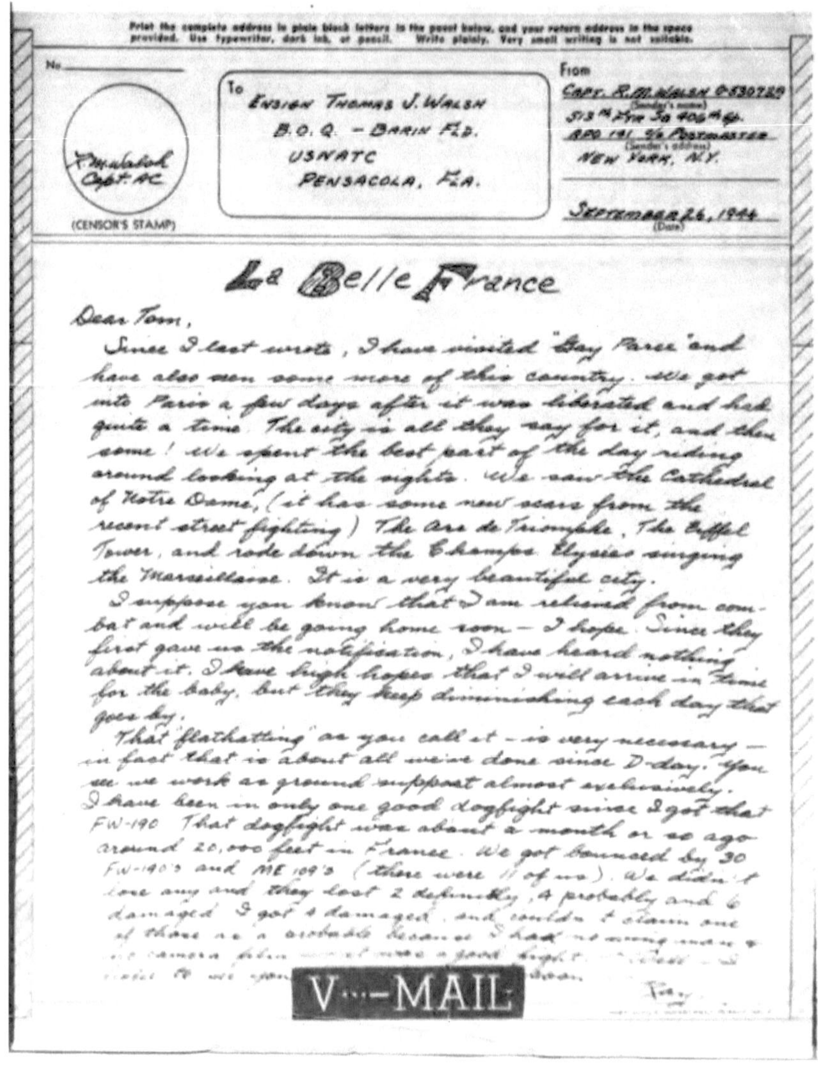

Print the complete address in plain block letters in the panel below, and your return address in the space provided. Use typewriter, dark ink, or pencil. Write plainly. Very small writing is not suitable.

No. ______

To
ENSIGN THOMAS J. WALSH
B.O.Q. - BARIN FLD.
USNATC
PENSACOLA, FLA.

From
CAPT. R.M. WALSH 0-530729
(Sender's name)
513th Ftr Sq 406th Gp.
APO 141 c/o Postmaster
(Sender's address)
NEW YORK, N.Y.

SEPTEMBER 26, 1944
(Date)

(CENSOR'S STAMP)

La Belle France

Dear Tom,

Since I last wrote, I have visited "Gay Paree" and have also seen some more of this country. We got into Paris a few days after it was liberated and had quite a time. The city is all they say for it, and then some! We spent the best part of the day riding around looking at the sights. We saw the Cathedral of Notre Dame, (it has some new scars from the recent street fighting) The Arc de Triomphe, The Eiffel Tower, and rode down the Champs Elysées singing the Marseillaise. It is a very beautiful city.

I suppose you know that I am relieved from combat and will be going home soon – I hope. Since they first gave us the notification, I have heard nothing about it. I have high hopes that I will arrive in time for the baby, but they keep diminishing each day that goes by.

That "flathatting" as you call it – is very necessary – in fact that is about all we've done since D-day. You see we work as ground support almost exclusively. I have been in only one good dogfight since I got that FW-190. That dogfight was about a month or so ago around 20,000 feet in France. We got bounced by 30 FW-190's and ME 109's (there were 11 of us). We didn't lose any and they lost 2 definitely, 4 probably and 6 damaged. I got 4 damaged and couldn't claim one of those as a probable because I had no ammunition & no camera film ...

V---MAIL

Dear Tom,

Since I last wrote, I have visited "Gay Paree" and have also seen some more of this country. We got into Paris a few days after it was liberated and had quite a time. The city is all they say for it, and then some! We spent the best part of the day riding around looking at the sights. We saw the Cathedral of Notre Dame, (it has some new scars from the recent street fighting). The Arc de Triomphe, the Eiffel Tower, and rode down the Champs Élysées singing the Marseillaise. It is a very beautiful city.

I suppose you know that I am relieved from combat and will be going home soon—I hope. Since they first gave us the notification, I have heard nothing about it. I have high hopes that I will arrive in time for the baby, but they keep diminishing each day that goes by.

That "flathatting" as you call it—is very necessary—in fact that is about all we've done since D-Day. You see, we work as ground support almost exclusively. I have been in only one good dogfight since I got that FW-190. That dogfight was about a month or so ago around 20,000 feet in France. We got bounced by 30 FW-190's and ME-109's (there were 11 of us). We didn't lose any and they lost 2 definitely, 4 probably and 6 damaged. I got 4 damaged, and couldn't claim one of those as a probable because I had no wing man & no camera film—it was a good fight. —Well—I hope to see you soon. -Ray.

The "flathatting" he refers to meant flying just above the treetops to watch the movement of troops on the ground.

A military service record for Raymond posted on American Air Museum lists an enemy aircraft destroyed by Ray over Germany on July 4, 1944.*

That makes three award-worthy actions in just his first few months. By the end of World War II, Ray had flown 75 combat missions, earning 17 air medals and 3 Distinguished Flying Crosses. He was decorated in France by Lieutenant General Omar Bradley and was widely known and respected as an elite "Flying Ace."

Our father took an active interest in his sons' military service. In 1944 Dad sent Rolex Oyster watches to each of his pilots—Ray in the Air Corps and me in the Navy. The Oyster was a very fine Swiss watch, watertight and shock-resistant, held in high regard.

Ray Aided in the Berlin Airlift

After the end of World War II, Ray continued to serve in the Air Force as a commissioned officer, but was moved into less perilous flying as a service pilot. Ray had a wife and two children by this time.

He was assigned to fly as a plane commander in the Berlin Airlift, where pilots were carrying food and supplies across Europe to the Allied groups. (The Berlin Blockade, which lasted from June 1948 to May 1949,

---

* Source: http://www.americanairmuseum.com/person/242482

Good-looking and a heroic flyer, Ray was chosen for publicity shots like this one about US participation in the Berlin Airlift. Possibly the actress is Ava Gardner.

was one of the first major international crises of the Cold War.)

Ray was featured in publicity about the US participation in the Berlin Airlift. On one occasion, a photo of Ray in his cockpit with an actress (Rita Stillwell? A young Ava Gardner?) appeared in the press.

Lost at Sea, 1951

Ray returned to the United States to fly for American Overseas Airlines (which later merged with Pan American Airlines) where he remained until he was recalled in 1950 to serve as a Senior Pilot Captain in the Korean War. He was made Wing Commander on a C97 Boeing Stratacruiser and assigned to Military Air Transport Services.

On a flight out of Lajes Field in the Azores, bound for Westover AFB Massachusetts, after radioing in one position call, his plane was never heard from again, lost in October of 1951. His route passed over what has been called the Bermuda Triangle. No trace of his aircraft or crew was ever found.

At the time I was flying a Cessna Twin Engine aircraft that had the same propeller connection as that C97. In manual inspection, my plane was discovered to have a cracked retainer ring on the propeller blades, and it was downgraded. I have in my possession that failed part, made by the same company that made the propellers for the Boeing airplanes Ray flew. Even though I carefully examined that retainer ring, even running a fingernail along it I can't find the flaw or crack that they determined was sufficient reason to condemn it.

I reflect on earlier experiences in transport air force when there were engine failures aloft, and recall the confusion about what happened and what to do. My theory is that a failed retainer ring caused Ray's plane to crash in the Atlantic without getting out a Mayday call and location.

Ray's death would indirectly lead to my career as a commercial airline pilot—but not before I served another stint as an officer in the NYCPD.

Chapter 5: Notable Police Stories

When you're a policeman on the beat in a major metropolis in the middle of the 20th century, the job demands readiness around the clock. It also calls for internal reserves of fortitude and integrity that will guide you to stand up and take action for what you believe is right.

Those were gifts my mother gave me, part of my DNA and my home training. They stood by me during the years from 1947 to early 1952, when I returned to the New York City Police Department after my stint in Owatonna, Minnesota with my Navy buddies, starting an airport. I was again assigned to the 9th Precinct on the Lower East Side of Manhattan, where I served under Inspector John Ferretti, 4th Division. This time I arrived a married man, for I had courted Martha Elizabeth Wesely while living in Owatonna. I went back to Minnesota for

Tom Walsh, New York City Police Department, about 1947.

our wedding. We started our married life in Long Island where we resided briefly in apartments before buying a home in Whitestone.

Initially, I worked the switchboard and other special assignments. Then I spent one year working as a plainclothesman in the 16th Division in Brooklyn. After that I went back to the 9th Precinct for a few months and then to the department's Emergency Services Division as a pilot. Many are my memories from that work, and the most notable police stories are included here.

A Lesson About Fire Alarms

In the early months of my 9th Precinct assignment, on the north end of the Bowery at about 4:30 AM just after the gin mills closed, I observed two men in a scuffle. They were at a corner fire alarm site pushing each other until one succeeded in pulling the handle on the box. Then amidst the loud clangor of bells and bright flashing red lights they started to flee the scene; one went toward me a half a block away on the other side of the avenue. The second one went the other way and was soon out of sight around the corner. I was thinking "false alarm" as I ran toward them and caught the one. I chased the first man down a short flight of steps near a building entry and gave him an order to stay there. I caught the other one, then brought both men to the corner and asked, "Where's the fire"? The pair silently exchanged regretful looks. Only seconds later police cruisers and fire engines, their sirens, bells and lights blazing, screamed onto the scene.

The fire department response in that high-vulnerability area was large, with aerial ladders, high pressure pumpers and other heavy equipment. There had been too many recent false alarms, including one where a fireman who responded fell from a speeding rig and died of the injuries he sustained.

After a brief exchange, several of the cops and firemen were swinging punches at my two captives, which obliged me to put both of my arms around the captives' heads while shouting, "Leave them alone, they're my prisoners." With that, the alarm box was secured, and I loaded my prisoners into a cruiser. We proceeded to the police station for booking. This crime ranked above the run-of-the-mill offenses brought before the Magistrates Court. Toward noon the two accused were arraigned in Special Sessions before a judge who was not at all pleased with my performance of my duties.

Fire headquarters had a staff attorney to assist in the presentation of evidence or any data the court might request. They had me sworn in on the witness stand describing the early morning incident. The judge asked me several questions: "Did you have a conversation with the accused? Which man activated the alarm?" I approximated the brief exchange and said I could not tell which one of the two men was the prime culprit. At that point the judge turned to me and with an air of kindly advice said, "Officer, a memorandum book is part of your duty equipment and wouldn't it be helpful to us if you would record there the details of these incidents so that you might properly testify in our courts?"

I sat there in silence thinking that this was another jurist hoping to be quoted in humorous comment or Solomonic judgment. I considered relating to the judge the details of what transpired on the streets of the city while he slept—and that making stenographic notes was not a high priority while capturing and holding miscreants.

The fire department official was quick to approach the bench and was heard to say, "That was an excellent and commendable arrest, and there is need for public shame of the accused." The judge quickly concluded the matter with a judgment of guilty and passed a rather severe sentence on the two accused. After that, I went home for some much needed rest.

Picketing Incident

One assignment sent me to the picket line of striking workers where by accident I was assigned a spot on the picket line in the area near the entrance to the company. A picketer there was unusually aggressive and was obstructing the passage of a young woman to her workplace in the building. He moved from side to side to impede her passage and lewdly accused her of working for 15 dollars a week to perform sexual activities for these employers.

When I observed him and heard his abrasive accusation, I stepped out of my picket line position and took hold of him and brought him to the temporary precinct inside the building. There, a captain sat in command with some lieutenants by his side. The captain said, "What do you have, officer?" I said, "I accuse this man of assault." The captain asked, "Where is the complainant?" I touched my finger to my chest and said, "I'm the complainant." The accused said he did not touch the young woman and I said, "He spat on her and accused her of sexual activities with her bosses inside." I pointed at the captain and said, "You would not tolerate such treatment of your wife, sister, or daughter, and neither would I." At that, the captain sent the prisoner to a holding cell, and told me to stand aside for a little bit. The captain had a conference with his lieutenants and assistants, and shortly after directed me to return to my precinct. I would not be needed there any longer that day.

I returned to the 9th Precinct and saluted the lieutenant at the desk, "Walsh back from strike duty." The lieutenant smiled and said, "Yes, we heard." He told me to go have a cup of coffee or something, and he would see what would be done next. But, as I left the front desk and walked away, the lieutenant said to the clerk, "There goes a priest." I was puzzled by that, but went on to the rest area. When I was called back a few minutes later, the captain told me I could remove my uniform jacket and weapons and stand beside the switchboard. I was to observe what the sergeant was doing there on the old-fashioned push, pull plug form of switchboard. After a few minutes of observation, the captain sent the sergeant to some other assignment. He told me to sit down and operate the switchboard. I did that on frequent occasions thereafter.

More Off-duty Action

When I was first with the NYCPD, I'd broken up a street fight while off duty (described in chapter 2.) Not long after my return to the police force, it became clear that any time of day or night, I might have to spring into action as an officer of the peace.

One summer evening I was walking from my car to a movie house with Martha, my pregnant wife, on my arm. She spotted an inebriated black man who was approaching from the opposite direction. We were on a wide sidewalk, passing seven or eight people in the waiting area of a bus stop. We walked along the curb. At the point when the man was about 10 to 15 feet away he began veering toward Martha. With a big grin on his face, he pulled up his shirt and made his exposed belly protrude over his belt, all the while continuing to move toward Martha. I didn't know if he intended to bump bellies or make a comparison with Martha's pregnant belly. No words were exchanged. He moved closer to Martha and gently stepped in front of her. When he did not stop, I smashed him in the face with my bare fist, and he fell to his side. At that point, Martha took my hand and we passed on our way.

A gentleman at the bus stop applauded my actions, saying, "Good boy, he deserved that." At the same time, my wife asked why I had done that, saying she thought we could have avoided the man. I politely replied that she had been greatly insulted in a public place, and my reaction was to protect and respect the tradition of motherhood. It also had to do with my work as a police officer. I was taught, growing up and through my work, to protect and serve. It paid off that night.

Another time when I was off-duty, driving along in my Long Island neighborhood, I saw a young woman on a porch with both hands up to her face. She appeared to be crying over something and in front of her, out on the grass, a big dog had her purse-sized little dog by the neck. He was shaking it back and forth as if trying to kill the little fellow. Without a second thought I stopped my station wagon and, reaching into the back seat, came up with a long-handled straw broom. I jumped out of the car and with a "Ted Williams home run swing" I hit the big dog across the side of the head. He dropped the little dog and turned away in response to a very convincing snarl from me. The young woman ran out and picked up her little pet dog and found him still alive and okay. She thanked me and I drove off. That was an example of the around-the-clock duty expected of a police officer. Animal or human, we protect and serve, any time, anywhere.

I Earn a New Assignment

After a couple of years in the 9th Precinct with a number of commendable arrests, I was assigned as a driver for our 4th Division Deputy Inspector. On an evening tour of our area, we heard an "assist patrolman" call. The Inspector and I were in the immediate vicinity and within seconds were the first responders on the scene.

An officer had apprehended a young punk in an assault and theft but was surrounded by an angry crowd pulling, pushing, and screaming insults in efforts to gain freedom for the captive. We screeched to a stop and went around the front of the vehicle. The Inspector was the "boss" out of the car and up on the curb saying, "Hold on there, we're the police...," but one of the rabble grabbed the Inspector's lapels and was about the shove him into the street. I took hold of the youth's collar and, delivering some street language the youth understood, heaved him back into the crowd.

Just then, two or three more police cruisers arrived. The officers dispersed the crowd and took the arresting officer and culprit to the station house. The Inspector and I dusted ourselves off and resumed cruising. My boss thanked me for my rapid assistance on the street. As the Inspector was speaking, I considered the notion that my boss, close to retirement, was too many years away from "hands-on" police work. I felt he was no longer in touch with the disrespect and rampant violence in the city. I assumed the Inspector went back and made a favorable report to his boss, the division commander, Inspector John Ferretti. Inspector Ferretti had seen reports of my police activities in earlier precinct reports. After that, I was assigned to drive Inspector Ferretti on several occasions when his regular driver was away.

A month or so after my evening with the Deputy Inspector, there was a plane crash in a densely-populated section of Queens. A Curtiss Commando World War II twin-engine transport (similar to the Douglas DC-3) that was being used as a freighter lost an engine on its climb from Idlewild Airport. It pancaked down on a busy street in Queens. The plane landed on top of two vehicles, one an unmarked police sedan containing the Deputy Inspector and his driver. The Inspector was killed; luckily the pilots and several other people on the ground were safe.

This was a very sad event for the Inspector's family. While policemen talk of perilous daily encounters in police work, this was a totally unforeseen event, "out of the blue" so to speak. No doubt I spoke about this incident, and others similarly perilous, with my wife Martha. Maybe this was the beginning of her concerns about my safety.

Another New Assignment: Undercover Work

Shortly after that event, I had occasion to express sympathy to the Inspector. He took the occasion to tell me he had some work for me.

He took me off regular uniformed work in our division and had me begin with wiretapping gigs. After a court order to the phone company, the police were given open access. The phone company directed the police to a junction box in the target vicinity as well as a number to identify the pair of terminals to clip into. In some instances, the junction boxes were 12 to 15 feet off the ground on telephone poles, and would make for conspicuous and awkward operations from the vehicle parked below. One early target of interest was a busy, off-track bookmaking parlor, which used an Italian restaurant as a front.

As part of my cover, I told the building superintendent that I was a phone technician. I situated my equipment in the basement of an apartment building two blocks away from the bookmaking parlor. From the vantage point of this building, I was able to gather much useful information on links to mafia operations. I also learned of the timing for a coordinated strike on the parlor's illegal gambling operation. We didn't use tape recorders at that time. We took notes on significant transactions and the timing of important activities. This helped coordinate our strike. In between calls relevant to the illegal betting there, I was privy to many details revealing the lifestyle of the mafia don who ran the parlor and its operations. There were conflicts between the don's wife and his mistress, and also struggles with his adult sons. It didn't paint a very wholesome or happy picture.

On an evening a few days before the planned police strike, I took my wife to the Italian restaurant for dinner. This enabled me to add faces to the voices I was acquainted with through listening in. I was not in on the action when my squad hit the place, but I was the one to notify the squad when the critical phone call came in. And in that way, I was the catalyst for the strike, which yielded a string of good arrests which in turn resulted in a serious shake-up of that crime syndicate.

Following that effort, the Inspector remarked that I could pass most anywhere "as a college boy in a turtleneck sweater with books underarm," and wouldn't arouse any curiosity. The Inspector had me scope out a site that our boss suspected of illegal activity. It was an exclusive bar/lounge in Midtown Manhattan that had earlier denied access to the boss's officers, the doormen saying it was a private club. The club was unlicensed, and it catered to an after-hours clientele, making it a police concern.

On my first attempt to get in I told them I had hoped to meet a friend. I was pleasantly turned away. On another occasion, I took a look at the rear of the building. At first as I entered the dark, deserted alley, I was unable to identify any access or exit options. But just then a janitor came out carrying refuse to the dumpster and was startled by my presence. I slurred my words and "drunkenly" said I had to take a p***. The janitor ignored me but didn't give me access to the building.

In the next week or so I focused on other places of interest, but prior to my next attempt to gain entry, I was given some advice by an old detective in my division. This guy had the trust of the Inspector and was aware of the current objective to get someone inside the club. The detective told me that the club was exclusive, and the only way I would get inside it would be to "pick-up" a "fairy" at one of the gay bars nearby.

A short time later at the Commodore Hotel in midtown Manhattan, I picked up a candidate who seemed well-informed on the places of interest, but couldn't be coaxed to leave the hotel. He only wanted a night there, with a Naval Lieutenant. I was recently discharged from the Navy, still active in the reserves, and looked like anything but a cop. Nonetheless, I had no success at the hotel nor in disguise at the club.

A week or so later it took me only a few minutes at a Greenwich Village hot spot to be observed and engaged in conversation by a likely candidate for my plans. I suggested that we go elsewhere for whatever might develop, and the prospect suggested we go to his car, which was parked close by. So we tucked ourselves into a little British convertible with the driver seated on the right side, and briefly chatted about where we might go. The prospect suggested that we go to his place, and I responded saying maybe later, insisting that I'd like to go elsewhere first, suggesting we go to a particular club on East 34th Street. The prospect said, "Hell no, someone else will try to take you home."

After a little more conversation, the prospect reached over me into the glove compartment and showed me a tiny derringer in the palm of his hand. He threatened to use it if I wouldn't be nice and go along with him. I waved the gun aside saying, "Put that charming little thing away before I shove it up you're a**." He petulantly responded, "That wasn't what I had in mind." I had no intention of swapping his likely arrest for felony possession of an unlicensed firearm with the opportunity to gain entry into his club. So I continued riding with the guy, talking in mild disagreement for a while. Eventually I got the guy to drop me off, saying I might look him up sometime. In another week the Inspector gathered a hit team and smashed into the place. They arrested several of the principals in the operation and closed the club.

When Things Were Slow

In our area, drug problems were minimal and there was little or no prostitution, but there were a few notorious hangouts (bars, movie houses, and subway toilets) frequented by homosexuals (they hadn't taken over that pleasant innocuous word "gay" as yet) seeking companions. These actions and solicitations were at that time illegal and, when we were not making sufficient arrests for other crimes, our Inspector would send us out in pairs to "bring in those dirty devils."

On one assignment at an infamous subway toilet, I was "the bait" and was approached by a young man of about age 20. While he was thinking of delights to come, I was considering Section 8, Paragraph 22 of the Penal Code. The young man's proposal quickly convinced me that he was committing the crime as described in the Penal Code.

Earlier day arrests for these crimes sometimes involved prominent individuals. In efforts to gain freedom and avoid the consequent public shame, some of the accused turned to hand-to-hand combat. In this instance after I identified myself and told the man he was under arrest. He went along with no resistance or protest and was booked at the local police precinct.

During the booking procedure before taking him for arraignment in Night Court, the young man expressed one small concern: Would this have any effect on his admission to college in the Fall? With some impatience I answered, "Perhaps.What college?" He said, "St. Mary's of Gethsemane in Kentucky." And I said, "Isn't that a seminary for candidates for the priesthood?" He said, "Yes!" and I replied, "Well, I hope so."

The young offender was brought before the bench. When the bailiff read the charges from the arrest affidavit , the judge asked how the young man pleaded. He answered, "Oh, I'm guilty your honor, just as the officer stated." The elderly judge frowned deeply, looked at this disarming young man and asked several questions, which the accused answered promptly:

"How old are you?"

"20."

"Any earlier occurrences? "

"No."

"Education?"

"High school."

"Who do you live with?"

"With my parents."

Then the judge looked down at his folded hands and after a long pause said, "I'm doing something very unusual. I'm rejecting your plea of guilty, and I will parole you in the custody of this officer. He will take you to your parents and inform them of the seriousness of these charges, and see that you get assistance and counsel before appearing in court in this matter." Then the judge turned to me and asked if I would do that and I agreed.

I awakened the parents at their home in a nice section of Brooklyn at midnight and presented them with their son. The father was a prominent street paving contractor, whose one brother was a state senator and another a monsignor in the Diocese of Brooklyn. To make a long story short, the dad's attorney was another state senator and there were many postponements in the courts until the case was called before an amenable judge. Before the hearing, held "in camera", someone from the district attorney's office contacted me asking if I'd go along with plans to "throw the case out due to insufficient evidence." I agreed, and the case was quietly handled, the records expunged.

The accused young man was not present at the final hearing, but a year later in another courtroom the man's attorney recognized me. He greeted me and shared that his ward was doing well in the seminary and looking forward to ordination in a year or two. My response was something like, "Oh shit, don't tell me." Then I thought of what my old Irish mother would say to me as a child (in regard to priests), "You dare not fault them for the hand of God has touched them."

Plainclothes Activity in Brooklyn

The plainclothes squad consisted of 12 men under the supervision of a lieutenant who reported to our Division Inspector. We were only concerned with violations of law in gambling, narcotics, alcohol, and "vice." We were free to operate anywhere within our division with minimal direction from supervisors except from the

Inspector, who wanted at least one arrest each day. In our busy area, there were usually several arrests by early afternoon.

That unofficial quota resulted in us having a daily rotation of a designated score team keeping track of which officers had made arrests. If by late afternoon there was nothing on the books, some would be obliged to stay on to make collars for easy infractions. These were numerous in our heavily populated area. In fact, we would keep some in mind when we were the score team for the occasions when not everyone had made the required arrest.

There was little to no narcotics activity but many alcoholic beverage violations. The then-illegal bookmaking crimes were common and received most of our attention. One of our senior members had a tip on a big-time horse racing bookmaker and his modus operandi. It was said that the bookmaker arrived at his home at the same time each afternoon with a large briefcase containing the day's action—the money and bets that had been collected. This information was quite detailed with an accurate description of the man and his car. It came to us from an informant said to be reliable and not from any complaint or official inquiry. It was also said that the briefcase would contain betting records showing tracks, races, bettor identities, and probably at least $100,000 in cash. We referred to informants like this one as "stool pigeons."

I worked with fellow officers in pairs forming a team of six for this operation. Our Lieutenant was not involved and probably unaware of the plan. It seemed that my partner and I were there as backup. We weren't told the details of the plans—details like moving the target or evidence from the nearby neighborhood of jurisdiction, or booking him in one of their division precincts.

I suspected that a "shakedown" for a sizeable portion of the target's reported daily take was in the script. I wanted no part of that. The street we were watching was a long cul-de-sac with a broad median lined with flowers, trees, and shrubbery. I noted two gardeners with rakes or hoes working half way up the block. Three of our team were in a parked car across the median from the targeted house, and two more were located at the turning curve of the cul-de-sac. They were the ones to make the "snatch." My car was parked off the scene a block away and I stood in shirtsleeves at a newsstand kiosk apparently reading the sports pages of a just-purchased paper but with the whole scene completely in view.

Just before the target's scheduled arrival, I observed four men in a black sedan make the circuit of the area. They received a wave and nod from the gardeners up the block. The men in the sedan cast a curious look at me as they exited the car. I concluded they were the "patsies" and it was time to blow the whistle on the operation with the agreed-upon signal. I promptly folded the paper, drew a big white handkerchief, wiped my nose and turned to walk away. Looking back I saw the "big-time bookie" arrive and get out of his Caddie with briefcase in hand, waiting to be grabbed. The two cars with plainclothes men in them rolled slowly by as the gardeners dropped their tools and watched. The police left the locale and rendezvoused in their own area at a bar and grill, which was the unofficial meeting place away from division headquarters. The lead man said that "it stunk" and agreed that the operation looked too good to be true. They were afraid that it was a trap set to catch cops, not bookies. All commended me for my timely signal.

At that time the District Attorney's office had a deep investigation in progress looking for payoffs by the crime syndicate's gambling operations to dirty cops. In this inquiry (or witch hunt, as the patrolmen called it), all officers on plainclothes assignment were summoned before a grand jury and required to answer an extensive questionnaire accounting for every dollar of income and spending in the previous five years. That covered homes, autos, vacations, clothing, jewelry, gifts, second homes, savings and securities investments, and other things one might overlook. The plainclothesmen came through that check unscathed, but it seemed to me that on this occasion the mission was not the wholesome operation suggested. In the first place, our team was just one block outside their division boundaries. While as peace officers we were authorized to make arrests anywhere in the state, the information we acquired should have been given to the neighboring division within whose jurisdiction a crime might occur. In court testimony several months later it was revealed that there was a police unit involved in setting up entrapment scenarios such as described above. I thought, "talk about danger in police work, well, I guess so."

During the time of this assignment there was a citywide crackdown on illegal gambling, and the word got out to the underworld to cease and desist. The police were under close scrutiny by the mayor's office, officialdom, and sensational press. We'd be obliged to sweep the streets clean of minor offenders.

A week or two into this effort, I made an arrest of a street corner bookmaker. He was arraigned in Magistrates Court, pleaded guilty, was fined $500.00 and released. Then out of employment at his usual occupation, and with a family to support, this guy went back to work on the docks as a longshoreman.

Cops' Social and Domestic Life

Speaking of families to support, most of us cops had families at home as well. A group of us met socially, and included our wives. Whoever was hosting the get-together, the first thing the host would do was put the guns in the freezer. We weren't allowed to get them until departing for home again.

We'd entertain ourselves with singing and some drinking to loosen our voices—there were several very good singers in the collection. We'd sing Irish ballads and other songs while our wives would be in another room, having their own conversations. We men would talk about "the job" as we called it, unusual things that had happened, individual assignments, and so on. We all had families except one among us. He'd been married quite a few years, but didn't have any children. He was the subject of teasing at times: when was he going to report a pregnancy? We told him, "It makes a difference which way you put your shoes under the bed" and jokes like that. We all expected to raise families.

My wife and I were living in Queens, because the NYCPD required that police live in the city so our services were available 24 hours a day. I didn't mind; I liked the neighborhood, which was just 8 or 10 miles from where I had grown up in Long Island City.

I was able to buy a two-family duplex for us with the help of a low-interest loan, part of the GI Bill. We rented out the other unit to another family. Police work paid enough to support a family, but just barely. I was licensed to sell real estate at the time, and made some additional income outside of my police work that way. An attorney steered me into getting that license, and I made a few purchases, remodeled old homes in what free time I had as a policeman, which wasn't much, and sold them at a profit. I began to hear more from Martha about her discomfort with my dangerous line of work, maybe because she saw that I could earn money in other ways. Perhaps she failed to recognize that I felt my police work was a calling, a way to live up to my mothers' lessons that I should "serve and protect."

The Police and Racial Profiling

At this time the New York City Police Department and its patrolmen were occasionally accused of racial prejudice in the way they applied the appropriate laws and ordinances to situations on the street. We officers had to consider that legislators and their staff, with righteous motivation contrived and enacted laws that while of commendable intent, were also all too often unfortunately open to a variety of interpretations and enforcements.

There was an old saying then, "There is more law at the end of a policeman's nightstick than in all of the law books in the land." There comes to mind the response by Willie Sutton, when asked why he robbed banks. He, with some apparent amusement said, "Why, that's where the money is." In like manner policemen are asked, "Why are there so many blacks in our jails?" Our prisons are filled with the racial group that fits the police profile of a likely criminal. The result is a racial group of inmates in excessive proportion to their numbers in society.

In that connection, a few incidents come to mind. The commander of a Special Crime Unit (he was a police captain and an old friend) was asked to cooperate with an outfit doing a documentary video on crime in the city with reenactments. They proposed the filming of a late-night robbery of a white taxi driver at gunpoint. The driver was dropping off a black fare on a Harlem street. The documentary company was to provide the film crew, the cab, and the actors. My police captain friend said there was no need for actors—his unit would provide what was needed.

It all went off as planned. In the follow-up review the film producer had high praise for the police officer actors and especially the one who played the gunman-robber. The captain accepted these compliments with the correction that the robber was not a cop but a real crook, arrested on the scene, and a similar scenario could be produced on demand in the crime-rampant streets of Harlem.

I recall a brief conversation with a black schoolteacher while I was on a daytime assignment in Harlem. She said that it was the opinion of many that they would prefer to see a more patient, white officer intervene at the scene of a violent confrontation rather than a black one.

Contrast that with the occasion when I broke up a fight outside a bar on a Sunday afternoon. I was confronted by an angry black woman, who said she did not like the rude language I had used in directing the combatants away from the scene. She noted the number on my collar indicating that I was from a downtown precinct, implying I did not know how to address citizens in her community. She wanted my name, saying she would be in the mayor's office the next day and would lodge a complaint against me. I told her that all she needed was my shield number and added, "Give his honor my compliments, and say the cop in her complaint applied the law in Harlem the same way he does downtown." Of course that wasn't possible, but I wondered what she would have said if she had been present a month or so later for a memorable incident during a period of violent protest in the city.

Harlem had had an increasing amount of vandalism, looting, and burning going on nightly. I was assigned as part of police reinforcement and was riding "shotgun" in the sidecar of a police motorcycle driven by my partner, a young black officer. The first five hours of my shift were reasonably quiet but around ten o'clock that July night, the radio dispatch called my partner and me. The dispatcher directed us to an address close by. A black man was on the roof shooting at lighted windows below and across the inner courtyard.

The location was remarkably accurate, and my partner and I followed the unneeded suggestion that we go quietly, as backup was on the way. The building was one of a block of four- and five-story tenements with fire escapes, stoops out front, and no access to the inner courtyard except through the lower floor hallways. My partner and I jumped out of our vehicle. He suggested that he'd take the fire escape. I gave him a leg up from the top of the front stoop to the bottom rung of the ladder and then ran for the inside stairs up to the roof. Once past some obstacles in the top-floor hallway, I came out onto the roof to see my partner seizing the shooter and about to throw him off the roof down to the street below. I tackled the pair. As they struggled to their feet, my partner shouted, "What the hell are you doing? He's no f*****g good, and we can't waste time in court with him just to see him out here again next week."

My partner's attempt may have been an example of street justice administered by black on black. It surely convinced the young culprit that he almost lost his life in his foolish escapade. Had I been first on the scene and attempted the same scare tactic, it would have been deemed a racial assault and the subject of severe criticism. We collected the rifle and other evidence, and took the young man down to the station for processing.

Assigned a Partner with Questionable Ethics

Within the Brooklyn Waterfront Division there were 12 cops who were from various parts of the city. Several were skilled in arts useful in their trade; one could pick locks quickly with hairpins, paper clips, blades, and such; another had a way with angry dogs, and could quiet them with a few words and a sniff of some "potion" he carried; others had been recognized for their ability in artful persuasion, physical or otherwise. My talents were in the latter area.

At one of the early gatherings of the 12, someone asked the question, "Who's your rabbi?" meaning who was the high command appointing you to this job for which there was no testing. When asked this, I answered, "I have no rabbi, but they [the high command] wanted someone with some balls." That drew smiles and no further questions.

My partner was a few years my senior and had undercover experience in other sections of the city. He was a good tutor in regards to arrests, evidence, testimony, and court procedures, but was known to bend the truth a bit on the witness stand. One of his eyelids drooped, and this had a disarming effect, making him seem the soul of sincerity when defense attorneys and judges questioned the truth of his accounts. He would say to me, "We all know that they're guilty, we just have to tidy it up a bit." He would suggest to first-time offenders that they plead guilty and throw themselves on the mercy of the court.

There was a bookie on the waterfront who managed to evade apprehension for a long time. He was on the docks in a secure area visible from the street through a high wire fence as he recorded betting information on tiny paper scrolls, which were later inserted in capsules attached to his homing pigeons' legs, and placed in a crate nearby. In the late afternoon he'd release the birds to fly to his home, and he'd depart the area free of any incriminating evidence. Since my partner and I couldn't gain access to the target area without causing an alarm, we came up with a plan where I toted a battered lunch box and dressed in denims, a jacket, and a longshoreman's cap.

Thus prepared, I got onto a neighboring pier, crossing the water between the gangways and barges to come in on the target a few minutes into the mealtime work break. As I sat on a crate and began to eat my lunch from the pail I carried, I saw the bookmaker we were seeking about 20 feet away, busily handling customers. I also kept my partner, who was in a car outside the fence, in view.

On a signal from the street to make the arrest, I abandoned my lunch and walked over to the bookie. Instead of money and a bet, I showed the man my badge. He immediately snatched up his tapes, stuffed them in his mouth, and swallowed them. By then my partner had forced his way through the street-side security and came to help. He was there in time to see the man consume the evidence, and said, "No sweat; we can write paper as fast as he can eat it."

My testimony in court for that arrest did not fit my partner's plans. I refused to present my partner's contrived paper scrolls, but accurately described the arrest scene and the disposal of the major evidence by the accused. On a motion of the defense attorney, the charges were denied and the case dismissed. My partner said he wasn't surprised, and said that we'd be under suspicion of taking a bribe for presenting insufficient evidence. I maintained that my statements under oath would continue to be nothing but the truth. We two continued as partners and cooperated in many fine arrests. We continued amiably, but with some areas of disagreement.

Although the department's rules of conduct required police officers to bear arms at all times, even off duty, my partner—for unexplained reasons—never had a gun on him or in his car. On a night when we were the score team, we were just about to pounce on a roving crap game when my partner said, "Here's the plan: you pull your gun, and we'll grab all of them."

I replied, "No, you don't have that right."

He responded, "Well, how many are you going to catch?"

With my arms extended, palms up, I said, "As many as I can hold with these two hands. I'm not about to shoot someone for rolling dice or sassing me." We got about eight men, and hauled them into the patrol wagon. We took them to night court, where they were fined and released.

At the Extreme—a Communist Police Officer

A fellow officer from a neighboring precinct was off-duty on sick leave. The sick leave rules only allowed him to be away from his home for medical reasons or to visit the doctor. He had been at a bar for several hours, and, after taunting a uniformed U.S. Navy sailor with grossly anti-American statements, was ejected from the premises. On the sidewalk outside, he continued the argument. A short distance up the street, a sanitation truck with a team of three were picking up garbage. They observed the man pull a gun and shoot the sailor two or three times. The man then threw the weapon down a nearby storm drain and started to flee. The sanitation men caught and held the man for the police who were responding with an ambulance. The sailor was critically injured and taken to Bellevue Hospital where he was treated for a couple of weeks and eventually recovered.

The delinquent cop was not originally from America, but had come to the U.S. with his parents from Poland at the age of 14. His parents became U.S. citizens but later returned to their homeland. The young man remained in the U.S., finished high school, worked at various jobs, and studied and trained successfully for the police exams. He went on to take the policeman's oath, and that oath charged him to uphold the U.S. Constitution and the laws of the State of New York. After his arraignment, he was sentenced to a year and a day in the state prison. Investigation of his record exposed that he was active in the Communist Party.

A Brush with the Mafia

During the time I was doing plainclothes work for NYCPD, the five-year-old son of a politically prominent family was kidnapped. There was an assumption that the family would receive a ransom message soon after the child was abducted. Public notices were posted requesting the ransom terms, and assuring payment at a site free of police surveillance. But four to five days of anxious waiting brought nothing but increased public and private concern.

Someone high in the police command structure decided it would be helpful to obtain assistance from the underworld crime syndicate, and after a brief period of cooperative inquiry, my partner and I were sent to meet a mafia leader.

We met the leader, the "Boss," in a private reception room at the rear of a lavish restaurant. We were greeted without any names or identification, seated at a table and offered drinks of our choosing from a well-stocked bar. This all happened before we proceeded to the purpose of our visit.

We were at a long table with the Boss at the head. My partner and I were seated on the right side. On the other side was a bodyguard or perhaps the Boss's son. After finishing with casual pleasantries about the weather, my partner asked the critical question as to their findings. The Boss had his hand up to his head and paused to consider his reply. Then suddenly the man on his left started to answer the question. The Boss mildly rapped him in the mouth and said, "I answer the questions here." The young man dropped his head. I felt the impulse to smile but thought that might be inappropriate. The Boss told us that after considerable inquiry over the last few days, reaching out to five neighboring states, he had no good information for us. He paused and told us he believed this crime was the act of a deranged person or sexual predator, and it was unlikely the boy would be found alive. We thanked him for his assistance and departed for headquarters.

Some four days later the police found the body of the young boy in an abandoned warehouse where he had been molested and killed. We were gravely concerned and felt deep sympathy for the parents and community over this tragic event. We also found it remarkable that we could accept the cooperation of the underworld in the investigation.

Is There a Right Time For Disobedience?

One incident demonstrated my character trait of doing what I thought was right—even if, at times, it meant acting in violation of an ordinance or a command.

There were four bridge connections between Manhattan and Long Island, three connected Manhattan and Brooklyn. At 59th Street there was a bridge over the East River, and at that point in the river the bridge passed over Roosevelt Island, where jails, hospitals, and other government buildings were located. Connecting the bridge deck to the island was a tower containing a vehicle elevator. A police officer controlled traffic to the elevator.

One day when I was hurrying to avoid being late to my downtown precinct, I was the first car in the westbound lane stopped at that intersection for an arriving ambulance arrived to use the elevator. The policeman had stopped traffic but now, there was no reason to be further delayed. I was impatient. The officer's demeanor said he was quite important to the progress of civilization, but I felt differently. *Just change that light and let me get out of here!*

My car had a manual gearshift and, in my impatience, I rocked the car back and forth in low speed. I observed that the cop had noticed. He was going to be really nasty and keep our lane stopped even longer. So, I just took off out of there. The officer blew his whistle and rang an alarm on the other side of the bridge, but what could he do?

I sped down the ramp and around onto the Brooklyn side and didn't give the incident any further thought. It was an example of my determination to act in order to achieve whatever I quickly determined was the proper action. And I succeeded in that attitude on many occasions.

Flying for the NYPCD

In 1949 I was assigned to the Police Aviation Bureau, Emergency Services Division, as a pilot. I flew Grumman Widgeon and Goose and Bell 47D helicopters. I got my multi-engine and instrument ratings during this period. I flew with a fellow patrolman, Gerald O'Rourke who was a graduate of Fordham University and law school. He was an ex-Navy pilot also. The purpose of the police aviation unit was to patrol the vast array of waterways around New York City, looking for thieves, stolen watercraft, and possible drowning victims. Sometimes we were directed to a scene to make observations.

Tom Walsh, pilot flying for NYCPD aviation unit providing emergency services, 1950.

One time, we were called to the scene of a would-be suicide on a bridge deck over the East River. It turned out that our hovering helicopter deterred him in his imminent plan to jump to the river below. He backed off from the rim of the bridge until police on the ground at the scene grabbed him and put an end to his attempt.

At about that time a renovation operation was underway on the steeple of St. John the Divine Episcopal Church in upper Manhattan. A carpenter up high was injured, and the rescue plan was to let him down to the street in a sling to the ambulance below. But he violently protested about the precarious descent on ropes, so one of our helicopters flew in and landed on the scaffolding and picked him up and dropped him down to the street. That and other rescue operations required precision flying by the copter operator. I was the copilot in some of these endeavors.

Disobedience on the Air Field

One time, I was given a flight plan to pick-up the mayor and the police commissioner at LaGuardia Field, Gate 1, 10:00 o'clock in the morning, and take them to Albany, the New York state capital. My copilot and I took up position in a spot that was the closest entrance for vehicle access. The tower sternly told me us to vacate that spot. It was reserved for an airline. I responded with, "No, we have authority to be where we are, to pick up the mayor and police commissioner." But the tower came back with another stern command to move our plane.

The mayor and police commissioner were close to arriving with their motorcycle escort. My copilot and I were told we were in serious trouble and were already held in contempt with Federal Aviation Association authority. We continued to defy the tower orders. Soon, our VIP passengers arrived and once they boarded, we departed for Albany. There were no actions taken against me or the copilot.

Retrieval of the Helicopter in the Bay

When I was assigned to the Aviation Bureau, it was noted in my record that I was an expert swimmer. When it happened that a report came in of a police helicopter that had crashed into the bay and was upside down in the water with only one float still inflated, no doubt those swimming skills were a factor in why I got a phone call from the police force's Marine Division. They called me and another officer to duty to help get the wrecked helicopter from the water so it could be taken to Floyd Bennett Field. Our job was to attach the tow line to a marine launch so it could be towed to a nearby pier.

Once at the pier, we were to meet a truck-borne crane which was to pull the wreckage out of the water. A hook was dropped down into the water and the other officer, Tony, and I used ropes to secure the chopper and attached the hook to the helicopter so it could be lifted from the water. We two swimmers were "manning the lines" that were keeping the chopper from hitting anything as it was lifted. When it rose from the water, the wreckage leaked some of its remaining 100-octane fuel, and it made a slick, highly flammable film on the surface of the water.

There were eight or 10 onlookers on the pier along with some uniformed police and others. An official in street clothing was smoking a cigar, standing next to the police captain. We looked up and observed this, and Tony yelled, "Hey you with the cigar! Get the hell out of there. Now!" The official asked the police captain if that was one of his men, and he replied, "Yes, and you'd better do what he's commanded you to do." Ultimately, they got the chopper safely onto a trailer for transport to a site for crash evaluation.

Flying Margaret Bourke-White

About the time of that "cigar incident," the NYCPD made an appeal to the city of New York to purchase more helicopters. There was a big stink in the press about the cost of the helicopters and so on, which led the world-famous photographer, Margaret Bourke-White, a staff photographer for *Life* magazine, to ask for help from the police to do a story showing the value of police aviation. She got the permission of the mayor and the city council to do a photo study of the New York harbor and waterways. I was assigned as copilot on a police helicopter for her flight.

She arrived equipped with three or four heavy, professional cameras. The plan was that during the flight, she would stand on the starboard-side pontoon wearing a tight-fitting harness attached to me, and I would keep her from falling and hand her various camera equipment as she called for it.

We took off and started with close-up pictures of the Statue of Liberty on Bedloe's Island. We flew close up to Miss Liberty's face, high above the water in the harbor below. She was leaning out and I had a firm hold on her harness, with the thought that if she went down in the water, I would go too and help her. Remember, I was known by the aviation department to be an expert swimmer. This shows my feelings about flying—I simply did not have any fears about it. Not takeoffs and landings, not even standing out on a pontoon, even with the possibility I might fall nearly 300 feet into the harbor!

A photo by Margaret Bourke-White taken from my NYCPD airplane.

Source: https://time.com/3879628/air-america-picturing-the-united-states-from-above/

When Bourke-White's photo-essay was published in *Life* I put it aside to save, but it has gotten lost over the intervening years.

It Was Leaving Time

I spent 1950 in the air over New York for the NYCPD Aviation Unit. A lot happened the following year—my father died of a heart problem on March 1, 1951. My wife gave birth to Thomas Daniel (Dan)—our first child, on May 17. My brother Raymond was lost at sea lost in October.

Dan's birth had not gone smoothly. He was impaired physically and mentally by an impatient obstetrician who used forceps to speed up the delivery. That made a big indentation on the side of the baby's skull, resulting in entire left side paralysis and some mental disability. My wife and I devoted time to looking for medical help for Dan. I remember spending time crawling around on the floor with Dan, trying to achieve the recommended exercises. There was no kindergarten in town, so he started school with the first graders, but was required to repeat the year. Later, we took him to Mayo Clinic in Rochester, where they lengthened tendons in his left side so he could grasp a steering wheel when he was old enough to drive. We engaged him on what was called the Dolman Delicado physical therapy treatment to achieve some utility, with the help of an operation run by a nun in St. Paul. Many observed that Dan's treatment was well-regarded.

After my brother Ray's disappearance, I went down to Miami to the headquarters of Pan American Airlines—Ray flew for a support airline contracted by Pan Am—to talk to the chief pilot about the odds of Ray's surviving. After he replied, he added that Pan Am had a team searching the country for pilots to hire. I told him I was a pilot—and that I'd flown under just about every bridge around Manhattan. With my experience, he said, I might fill in the need for more pilots at that time. It was a job offer!

For a long time, Martha had been growing more upset about the effect of my work on our family life. I was required to be on duty or active standby for 24 hours a day. My duty shifts called for work at all hours. It was expected that we would take part in any and all incidents happening. No doubt her worries increased after Dan was born.

By this point, she was terribly set against my continuing the police work. I would have liked to stay with it. But, to keep the peace at home, when the Pan Am opportunity came along, the decision was easy. I loved to fly, and it would please my wife.

I resigned from the NYCPD on February 18, 1952 and went to work for Pan Am. In fact, there was an occasion when a neighbor lady said to my wife, "Aren't you worried, now that he's doing this dangerous work, flying for Pan American?"

She replied, "Oh no, it's not like when he'd come home with his clothing torn or bloodied."

The job change proved to be a good one. I didn't have to move my family from our neighborhood in Queens; we could stay right there. I remained with them until September 1, 1953. It was a short but interesting period in my career.

Chapter 6: Flying for Pan Am, 1952–1954

In 1952, when I was 34, I was recruited from the New York City Police Department to fly for Pan American World Airways (Pan Am). Here's how that happened: Several months after the loss of my brother, Raymond, I visited the headquarters of Pan Am in Miami, Florida in regard to my brother's affairs, since they had been his employer. (Ray was survived by his wife, Isla, then 7 months pregnant, a daughter, Celia, and a son, Kevin.)

I met Pan Am's chief pilot, who was aware that I was a pilot of some experience. He said, along with condolences about Ray, that they were in the midst of a countrywide search for pilots qualified for careers with Pan Am. I told him I had the ratings needed, but that most of my flying hours were in single-engine planes. He said they were very interested, gave me an application form, and two weeks later I passed the physical.

I resigned from the NYCPD on February 18, 1952. My first day as a Pan Am pilot was March 4, just over two weeks later. It was fitting that I should work for Pan Am, since my childhood hero, Charles Lindbergh, had served as Pan American Airways' technical advisor.

At some time in my probationary period, Pan Am's chief pilot called me in to explain an item I had inserted in their new-pilot application. There was a large blank space on that old, unrevised form which asked, "Any unusual exploits in aviation?" From a long time back, I'd had the peculiar habit of injecting humor into serious situations and giving sometimes other-than-obvious answers to ambiguous questions. Not having any "farther, faster, or higher" claims, I answered somewhat fliply, "Well, I have flown under most of the big bridges around New York City." I was back in his good graces upon telling him of normal police operations in our amphibians and helicopters looking for stolen small craft, drowning victims, and other marine disasters.

Here, There, and Everywhere: All in a Day's Work

A Pan Am flight crew consisted of a Captain (the pilot), First Officer (the copilot), one or two flight engineers, and sometimes a navigator. The flight engineers might be qualified pilots, but their responsibilities were fuel management and other related tasks. Their presence

While with Pan Am I flew Douglas DC3 and DC6B planes like this one.

provided backup, should something go wrong with pilot and copilot. I most frequently served in the position of copilot.

Also onboard would be the stewardesses and a purser, a male attendant with basically the same role as a stewardess, taking care of passengers.

I started out based in New York at John F. Kennedy Airport (then known as IDL, or Idlewild). I received some instrument training in DC3s and checked out in Douglas DC6Bs. I was assigned to fly DC6Bs, mostly.

Later I was asked to move to London, to be based out of LON (Heathrow). My wife, Martha, and toddler son, Dan, came along, of course. We lived in London less than a year, but that was sufficient time to make friends and to enjoy getting to know the city. We spent Christmas holiday that year in Paris.

North, East, South, and West!

Frequently, while flying out of IDL my routes were to Western Europe with stops in Boston; Halifax, Nova Scotia; Gander, Newfoundland; Goose Bay, Labrador; and Keflavik, Iceland. We flew into Ireland, Scotland, England, France, Italy, Belgium, Holland, Germany, and the Scandinavian countries, with stops at most major European capitals.

Another route I frequently flew was via the Azores to Portugal, and then down the west coast of Africa by way of Lisbon, Dakar, Accra, Ghana, and Leopoldville in the Belgian Congo to Johannesburg, South Africa. I sometimes flew cargo-only flights in Atlantic crossings in Pan Am or Slick Airways DC6As.

After the move to London, I flew routes to Hong Kong via Frankfurt, Istanbul, and sometimes a layover in Beirut, Lebanon, then on to Basra, Iraq; Rangoon, Burma; and Karachi, Pakistan. We flew through several cities in India and on to Bangkok, Thailand; over Vietnam (then called French Indochina) to approach Hong Kong via the South China Sea (with daylight VFR—Visual Flight Rules—only).

I flew above the Arctic Circle to Kotzebue, Alaska and north of Iceland. I flew below the equator to South Africa, and east across Europe, and the Mideast, to Hong Kong. I flew west to Hawaii, Taiwan, Japan, Hong Kong, and into China. The farthest south I ever flew was Johannesburg, South Africa. I crossed the International dateline. Piloting for Pan Am took me here, there, and everywhere!

Pan American Airways had been a pioneer in long oceanic crossings with its worldwide meteorological reporting stations. It is notable that Pan Am had devised a so-called "pressure-pattern" flying system with much longer routings along the isobars (like swimming with the current) giving better trip times and fuel economies than the direct "as the crow flies" routes.

Take-offs, Approaches and Landings in Heavy Weather

Working for a commercial airline required that at times, I had to fly under extremely poor weather conditions. I have experienced successful approaches and landings at airports with little or no ceiling (the altitude at which the lowest clouds are visible) and visibility.

Heathrow on a Radar-Assisted Ground-Controlled Approach

Once, as a copilot with Pan Am, I flew into fogbound London's Heathrow airport on a radar-assisted GCA (ground-controlled approach). As a copilot, along with responding to approach control, it was my function to call out "ground contact" when the runway was in sight. The fog was so thick, we were below the 50-foot warning and beyond the threshold on the 8,000-foot runway before I could dimly see runway lights on my side. There was hardly any forward visibility. The controller talked the captain through touchdown and rollout to a taxiway where we were met and escorted to the ramp by a brightly lit "follow me" vehicle.

The British, having naught but distant foreign alternatives at which to land, became early innovators in radar and put it to good use at their fogbound airports. For much of my time as a pilot, we in the US restricted radar to military and emergency use only.

Landing a DC6 at Santa Maria, Azores in a Severe Crosswind

Another Pan Am landing comes to mind, again as copilot, I did not execute the approach. It was in a DC6B at Santa Maria in the Azores, on a westbound trip home from Europe. We had a "check captain" aboard on that crossing, making a detailed report on crew performance. He occupied the flight engineer's slot in the cockpit between our captain and me. The weather at the time was not ideal: ceiling at 400 feet, visibility half a mile in moderate rain, and a very strong crosswind. The captain said he'd make the ILS approach and that I would make the landing, calling out and taking control after positive visual contact with the runway. (ILS, or Instrument Landing System, is based on two radio beams that, together, provide pilots with both vertical and horizontal guidance during an approach to land.)

The approach was precise, and as we descended the last few hundred feet, I noted we were drifting increasingly to the right as our speed diminished. Either from instinct or from my light aircraft experience, I flared our nose high, left wing low, right rudder, and touched down lightly, left main landing gear first, then right main and nose gear along the centerline of the runway.

On rollout toward the taxiway our captain turned with a smile to the check captain saying, "What did I tell you?" In post-flight debriefing, there were remarks about too many young pilots planting planes like eighteen-wheelers or locomotives on the runways, with no regard for stress imposed on equipment. I responded modestly to compliments, noting several thousand hours of flight-instructor duty. I told them that, like baking cookies, "They don't all turn out quite right."

Shannon to Gander with Primitive Plane Controls

With that same captain on a later flight from Shannon to Gander, we encountered severe headwinds. We got clearance to descend to 200 feet above a turbulent sea, which for an airplane is practically on the surface. It was an extremely rough ride, all the way across the Atlantic at that low altitude. There was salt spray everywhere—on our windshield, on our wings.

We had no autopilot. We had no navigator—he and another crew member had become 'seasick' and were indisposed. They refused to come up to their flight positions—too worried that the plane might be knocked into the sea. With no one to relieve us, the captain and I handled the whole over-ocean flight by ourselves.

We had only primitive dead reckoning because we were forced to fly too low to use normal navigational aids. We got ADF (automatic direction finding) bearings from a radio beacon, homed in on that, and overflew our destination. I got a picture of USCG weather ship Charlie, "ON STATION" 800 miles off Newfoundland, with decks awash and a sick crew. Nobody was having a comfortable ride that day.

A month or so later, I was with the same captain and crew, preparing for a gate departure on a flight from IDL to Paris. The plane's first officer was scheduled to make the takeoff. Our captain arrived up front and summarily ordered that pilot out of the cockpit and back to join the cabin attendants. The pilot protested that it was his scheduled takeoff, but was rudely dismissed by the captain with the remark that Walsh would do the job. "He and I flew the Atlantic together," the captain remarked abruptly. He hadn't forgotten that rough crossing from Shannon to Gander either.

If It Isn't One Thing, It's Another

Approaches and landings aren't the only moments a pilot needs steady nerves and sterling judgment. There were a number of times mine were called to duty.

Lightning Strike

One sunny afternoon, we were approaching the Frankfurt airport when a line of thunderstorms moved across the destination airport. We were a few miles short of the initial contact with the ILS approach, flying at about 4000 feet, when we observed numerous lightning strikes. Suddenly there was a tremendous blinding flash of light and an explosion. There was a strong smell of ozone.

In my copilot seat, I wondered if we were destroyed. I felt my chest and limbs to see if my body was still there. I blinked my eyes to try and regain my vision. The captain said, "I think we're okay—don't change anything." As my vision gradually came back, it appeared that the instruments were telling us everything was normal—except for one compass that was spinning. There was static on our radio communications as well.

Then, following a careful assessment of all our systems, we determined we were safe and continued on our way toward the airport. We informed the approach control and tower of our shocking situation.

Not too long after the lightning bolt, our senior cabin attendant appeared at the cockpit door. She did not come forward, but tossed a roll of toilet paper above the dashboard beyond the windshield, saying, "Here boys, I think you might need this."

The captain barked back, "Alright smart-ass, get out of here."

We landed securely shortly after that. A thorough inspection showed paint loss on the nose of the airplane and a static whip burned off of part of the elevator. Other than that, no apparent additional damage to the airplane was noted. We had all seen what was called St. Elmo's Fire, but this was more than we'd like to see again.

Voice Communications and Vocal Registers

On a flight from the US to Europe, we were having great difficulty making radio contact with any ground stations near or far, due to sun spot activity. We could hear requests from Iceland, the Azores, Bermuda, Gander in Newfoundland, and others, asking for our position reports, now at least three hours overdue.

After many hours without success making radio contact, I recalled under similar circumstances having heard the only intelligible messages in lilting, high-pitched, Irish accents from the "colleens" at Shannon Oceanic Control. Everyone else on the air was unreadable gurgles and growls. Distance from the calling station did not seem to matter. Even though the Irish airport was the farthest away, I clicked on my mic and pitching my voice to a real high falsetto, I called Shannon. They answered immediately! We were pinpointed on their charts again. Meanwhile, our captain, observing my efforts, at first wrinkled his brows in disbelief and then, hearing the result, broke into a smile and nodded his approval.

Modern improvements to communications equipment can enhance delivery greatly, with volume—to the annoyance of many—and also with amplitude of bass tones to enhance the timbre of male voices. This last is overdone in many places and makes for unintelligibility, in my opinion. It results in sounds such as thimble fingers playing on laundry washboards. Perhaps some tweaking of the pitch/tone controls on equipment might bring about some better understanding of the messages and save patience all around.

Shannon and a Near-Death Experience

The Irish have a special way with words as well as an especially musical way of speaking. I'm reminded of a takeoff heavy with fuel in an old airplane from Shannon, Ireland bound for Boston. There was no wind and unusually high air temperatures, which made that old boat even harder to fly than usual. The flight engineer commented that it was a difficult climb-out, and the captain made a rebuttal, telling the flight engineer that he believed they would be able to make the climb and get out over the sea in cooler air to successfully complete the flight.

One engine conked out, so the engineer dumped fuel. The other passengers, noticing that the propeller was not turning, were troubled by an old Irishman on board who loudly proclaimed, "We're going to meet our God today." Thankfully, we didn't.

Language Games

There were two Pan Am captains of about the same age and background. They had developed a cordial relationship, and when they would meet, either one would say to the other, "Pass the foomer!" The other would reply, "Eat the cracker!" That was their version of the signs frequently seen in public places in France. The message was no smoking or spitting: PAS DE FUMER ET DE CRACHER.

This would remind me of an exchange that brother Raymond and I had used in similar fashion when we were growing up. It originated in the Italian neighborhood of our boyhood, and it went: "Hey, wallio! Kay sa deech!" And the response was: "Kay eh sa deech!"

"*Hey, jalio! Que sa dice! Que est a dice?*" would have been the Italian.

Long after my brother Raymond was declared missing in the Atlantic, I was on a flight along the Eastern seaboard and listened to a transmission from a military refueling flight. I was impressed with the similarity to my brother's voice, as I remembered it. I called out on the same frequency, using the old greeting Ray and I would exchange.

"Hey, Wallio….." the hair stood up on the back of my neck, thinking that I might get an answer. Sadly, no such result.

Drunk Passengers

For a while, when residing in London, I made a number of flights from London to Hong Kong with stops en route in Germany, Turkey, Beirut and other Near East ports. On one occasion, with me in the copilot's seat, we made a stop in Frankfurt, Germany. Four US Army colonels boarded who had been partying and weren't about to stop. They brought their own supply of liquor aboard, and, when the stewardess closed the cocktail hour for dinner, they continued to imbibe from their own supply.

On those long-range flights, our toilet accommodations were larger than the usual airline facilities the size of telephone booths. Each plane had a restroom for each gender, with double sinks.

The stewardess reported the troubling activities of these inebriated army officers to the captain. When he told her to close the Happy Hour, she reported that had already been accomplished. She went on to describe what happened next: One of the drunken officers had to throw up the contents of his stomach. He defied the seat belt sign and, as he proceeded to the men's room, sprayed some of the nearby passengers with vomit. He then refused to return to his seat.

The captain looked across the cockpit to me and said, "Hey, you're an ex-cop. Go get that bunch quieted down." He went on: "Get that fellow seated and tell him he is under arrest and not to leave his seat until I release him. If you have any trouble, holler out and the engineer and I will come help."

Thereupon, I went to the men's room and found the delinquent officer scrubbing the front of his uniform at one of the sinks in an effort to clean up. I pointed to the seat belt sign and told the officer that he was to go back and get into his seat. He said to me that he was not used to taking orders. I told him he was not in that position now.

The officer said, "Oh, you were probably one of my GIs in the recent military operations."

I said, "No, I was also an officer—a full colonel." I went on to tell him that he was a disgrace to the uniform he wore, not just in my eyes but to the many foreign nationals present on the plane. Thereupon, I grasped the officer by the shoulder and started him on his way back to his seat. I saw to it that he was tightly fastened in and told him not to get up again until the captain released him at the end of the trip. His fellow officers helped by cautioning him, and he submitted to our commands and directions.

When they were preparing to disembark at Istanbul in Turkey, after some mild apology from the officer to the captain, he was released.

Moving a DC6 Out of a Puddle of Fuel

I'm reminded of an incident with Pan Am in Africa when it was necessary to move (without motorized help) our DC6B out of a pool of spilled high-octane fuel with air temperature about 115°F. We had on board a young man, a polio victim in a complete body cast, as well as several infants and their mothers. The risk of that fuel combusting was high, and I was concerned for my passengers' safety.

We didn't dare start an engine for fear of creating an explosion. We had been offered a big tractor, but rejected that solution for fear of damaging our aircraft. Then our station chief summoned a group of black laborers who, scantily-clad as was their custom in the African heat, harnessed themselves to that plane with a long hawser. They began singing a native chant, leaned into the effort in unison, and got the job done in a short time. Plane, passengers, and pilot were safe to proceed.

On the Character of Some Pilots

On one occasion, I was copilot on a relief mission to Holland during a flood caused by a break in a dyke. We flew New York to Amsterdam loaded with first aid supplies and rescue equipment. When we landed, we unloaded it all, even boats to cope with the high water.

The pilot I was flying under was of a very different moral character than I. He liked to break the rules, from the regulations about flight paths to everyday etiquette. He was a radical and a lecher who pursued every female in sight.

After our work was done in Amsterdam, we were scheduled to fly down to Nice, France on the Mediterranean. He took us at low altitude all the way, just because he liked the challenge. As copilot, I had no choice but to perform my job and not criticize how this captain was violating regulations.

We made it to our final destination: Johannesburg, South Africa. When we were scheduled to depart for Lisbon, we had a full load of passengers and cargo. We needed a full load of fuel for the flight.

The stewardess could not legally close the doors as there were two extra passengers on board, a woman and her son. The captain proposed to fly them to a nearby airport. This stewardess said she couldn't sign the manifest with those two aboard. The captain told her, "Close the door. We're going anyway." The stewardess refused, saying she could stay behind. The extra passengers were treated to a circular flight around the city and then flown up to Johannesburg's alternative airport.

The woman passenger had a car and driver waiting to take her back to Johannesburg. She was the captain's lover for that weekend, thus such special treatment.

The Life of a Pilot

As pilots, our work life consisted of 12 to 15 days on duty, away from home. For our layovers, Pan Am had arrangements with various hotels to house its crews. The captain got an exclusive room. The first officer shared a room with other male personnel. Stewardesses roomed with each other. They weren't called flight attendants yet, and they were all female, young, single, and selected for their pleasant appearance, a calming presence to nervous flyers—or at least a distraction.

Flight schedules might dictate a very short layover for the plane's crew, sometimes just long enough to meet federal regulations for adequate rest. Other layovers might last several days, depending on the particular route. At the end of that roughly two-week tour of duty we might have one or two days at home and then we'd be off again. My family accepted that this was our way of life.

"The Campbells are Coming"

On one occasion in the summer of 1953, while on a Pan Am layover in London, I agreed to meet my niece,

Irene Wencl, at noon for lunch during her visit there. We agreed to meet at a café that happened to be below street level. There was a small orchestra at the bottom of the stairway entry area to the café.

I wore a sweater with a Scotch tartan pattern to our meeting. As I came down the stairs, the orchestra leader observed the Scotch family tartan and struck up the tune, "The Campbells are coming, tra la, tra la!". I descended the stairs, accepted their musical greeting with a big smile, and joyfully greeted my niece as we proceeded with our planned luncheon.

Not Your Usual Flight Attendant

During my stint with Pan Am based out of London, on one of those long cross-continent flights to Africa or the Far East, Betty Haas was aboard. Betty, the daughter of a wealthy New York department store owner, held an airline transport pilot certificate and in earlier years had flown an F51 Mustang in the Bendix Races (trans-continental, point-to-point races) with other famous women pilots. I always liked and respected her.

Even though she was an ace pilot, the best job she could get with the airlines in those days was as a cabin attendant. On occasion, she would come up to the flight deck to complain about turbulence, saying we were spilling the soup and should do a better job to make the flight smoother. She turned up years later—but that's a story for the next chapter.

Suspicious Behavior

On a flight from New York to Paris we were returning with a three-day layover in London. On that Paris-London flight, the crew's purser behaved in a way that triggered my "cop" instincts. At customs in London, we were asked if we were carrying any British currency. We each said "about 10 shillings"— which was typical. We just carried local currency for tips or whatever.

But this time, the purser said, "No foreign money."

"How much American?" the customs agent asked.

"One dollar," he replied. It amused me to think a guy would go abroad with one dollar in his pocket.

The customs agent asked, "May I see it?"

The purser refused to show it. That struck me as odd.

As it happened, the purser and I roomed together. We stayed in London for our three-day layover, but I didn't see hide nor hair of him during that time until the last day of our stay. He took his suitcase into the bathroom, where I observed him through the open door counting large sums—French francs, British pounds—and tucking them into secret pockets in his suitcase. He even tucked some into his boots.

Remember, this was in the middle of the 1950s, the era of Cold War hostilities. I came to the conclusion that the purser was a courier of some kind working for the communists. As a purser for Pan Am, he could pick and choose his routes—and so different destinations to deliver messages and money.

I got all the information I could about him. Once we got back to Manhattan, I went to the FBI headquarters and asked to speak to an agent. I shared what I had observed, what I had concluded, and suggested the FBI investigate that purser. The agent was very pleased to receive this information.

Secret Service Contact

During a Pan Am flight from London Heathrow to Hong Kong with a second stop at Beirut, Lebanon, I was replaced on the flight by another pilot. I was told to remain in Beirut for three days, until the next flight came through. On my first evening there, I went down for dinner in the Bristol Hotel where the company maintained quarters for their visiting crew. The maître d' sat me at a table for two, and a few minutes later asked permission to seat another man at the table with me for dinner.

The man who sat down was a tall, slim, young man dressed in Arab garments. He seated himself opposite me and proceeded to manipulate some beads in his

Archibald (Archie) Byrne from the St. Ann's Academy yearbook, Class of 1934.

hand. I asked if they were prayer beads, like Catholic rosary beads. The man responded in unaccented English, "No, they are just worry beads, like the beads Humphrey Bogart twirled as Captain Queeg, in the film *Mutiny on the Bounty.*"

That made me curious! I tried to distinguish some foreign accent in my companion's speech, but he truly sounded like an American from New York. I asked if he was familiar with Manhattan in New York City, and he nodded with a modest smile. I then asked him if he would give any thought to Lexington Avenue and 76th Street across the street from Lenox Hill Hospital, and the man smiled a little more broadly. I nodded yes, to indicate that we didn't need any further identification from each other. He had been one of my classmates in the St. Ann's Academy class of 1934—Archibald (Archie) Byrne. I suspected Archie had joined the Secret Service.

End of the Pan Am Years

I flew for Pan Am for only a couple of years, but it afforded me the opportunity to visit exotic places unlike anything I'd seen before. Many of the cities we flew to in those years were in undeveloped countries compared to the US, the UK, and western Europe. In French Indochina (now Vietnam) we saw traditional sampan boats used for transportation and habitation in the harbor. In the Belgian Congo on the west coast of Africa, we saw young women carrying infants on their backs while balancing baskets on their heads as they walked. It often seemed we were flying not just around the world, but back in time.

In the spring of 1953 I was transferred back to New York and continued flights to Europe and South Africa. I had longer layover time at home, and became licensed in real estate. In response to pressure from Martha who wanted me out of police work, we had agreed that a combination of flying for Pan Am and real estate activity offered a safe alternative.

It was late 1953, I was in Whitestone in Queens, New York, selling real estate, and expecting this to be my next endeavor for some time. I was purchasing properties, rehabbing them, and reselling them, doing some of the work myself and hiring contractors for certain specialized work. I had begun doing what today we'd call house-flipping, toward the end of my employment with the NYCPD in the late '40s. With increasing success in real estate, I supplemented Pan Am's modest salary.

Then Pan Am furloughed 150 low seniority pilots, including me. After further cutbacks at Pan Am, I separated from the company on July 19, 1953. I began full-time real estate sales in Whitestone, New York. While I was showing houses, a new opportunity knocked.

Chapter 7: Back to Owatonna to Work for Jostens 1953–1970

After the Navy but before flying for Pan Am, I had spent few months in Owatonna, Minnesota with my friends Glenn Degner and Joe Dulak getting a new commercial airport off the ground. In 1953, a job offer called me back to Owatonna.

When looking for a temporary place for our airstrip operation, we had contacted Terry Cashman, the owner of some suitable land west of Owatonna. Terry's cousin Betty Cashman was a part-owner of the land we had in mind. She was married to Walter Gainey, who was the brother of Daniel C. Gainey, who happened to be the CEO of Jostens, a manufacturer in Owatonna.

When the Gainey brothers began asking around about pilots, my association with the Owatonna airport led the Cashmans to recommend me. Walter Gainey phoned me to say Jostens had just bought an airplane and wanted someone with commercial airline experience to fly for them. I talked it over with Martha. She welcomed the idea of a steady job for me and a return to Minnesota with our growing family.

I accepted the Jostens offer with great enthusiasm. Martha, pregnant with our second child, flew back to Minnesota with our son Dan in early October. I put our house in Whitestone, New York up for sale and followed by car with some of our belongings. On October 22, 1953 I began my employment with Jostens as Chief Pilot.

Our daughter Mary Pat was born on January 1, 1954 at St. Mary's Hospital, Rochester. A month later, Gerald P. O'Rourke bought our house at 20-44 150th Street, Whitestone, NY for $13,200. That was $3,000 more than we paid for it.

Jostens Chief Pilot, Tom Walsh

My title at Jostens might as well have included Chief Cook and Bottle Washer, as I was the only pilot when I started. All duties related to aviation fell to me.

The easiest way to explain what Jostens did is to say that they made and sold the stuff that helps people celebrate achievement. An Owatonna jeweler/watch repairman started the company in late 1897. He began with products for high schools and colleges, such as yearbooks and jewelry. Dan C. Gainey had gone to work for the company in 1922 as the first Jostens ring salesman. The company quickly grew to include sports and corporate markets as well, and within one year he had grown his department to five salesmen. In 1930, the watch repair business was sold and the proceeds used to build a manufacturing plant for Jostens. In 1933 Dan C. Gainey was elected chairman and CEO. According to an online history of the company, "...Gainey's greatest contribution to the company was his establishment and motivation of a nationwide sales force. Direct sales through independent representatives remain the primary source for the company's virtually uninterrupted growth."

By the time I was invited to join Jostens, the company had a separate yearbook publishing division in addition to its manufacturing operations. More companies serving national markets were shifting from commercial air travel to owning their own planes. Jostens was early to join that trend. Jostens had purchased a Beechcraft Bonanza, regarded as the Cadillac of single-engine aircraft at the time. As Chief Pilot it was mine to fly.

The company grew into new markets and more plant locations, which allowed us to expand flight

Group of pilots in the early 1950s. I am second from right (in bow tie).

Group of pilots from a Learjet training about 1963. I am second from right.

operations to three airplanes: the original Beechcraft Bonanza, plus a twin-engine Cessna 310 and a second Bonanza. We employed five pilots. We flew corporate and government VIPs to destinations all over the US and Canada. (More about that to come later in this chapter). I developed a great respect for Dan C. Gainey and understood that he held me in high regard as well.

After several years of flight operation, Jostens had grown from a country ring store to a national distributor of engraved watch cases, rings, and trophies. Dan C. Gainey saw the need for more advanced aircraft that would enable longer flights to reach distant small airports and to fly through bad weather conditions which usually grounded our small planes. I suggested that he consider the newly operating Learjet 24B. Gainey's response was immediate and strong: "No. That would be too expensive." I showed him comparisons of the initial airplane cost as a share of total assets, and also the cost of the Learjet as a share of current assets, demonstrating that the higher initial cost was more than made up over time in the greater efficiency of the modern jet. When Dan saw the exact ratio of values, he said, "We are going to buy that Learjet." He was opposed in this decision by Charlie Oswald, one of several young Harvard Business School graduates to join the Jostens executive suite, but Dan went ahead anyway. Jostens purchased a

Learjet Model 24B in which I earned type-rating and logged 700+ hours. I had many interesting and memorable flights before retirement in 1970.

While Flying For Jostens

During my just-under-seventeen years with Jostens there were many good (or at least exciting) experiences, and I will tell some of them now.

Hello, Betty Haas

While flying for Jostens with Ole Olson, a sales manager visiting some of his southern sales force, we encountered a line of thunderstorms that forced us to take shelter at the Shreveport, Louisiana airport. We were directed to taxi the plane right into a big hanger behind other live aircraft already secured there. The big doors were closing behind our plane as the storm closed in on us across the field beyond the runway. I thought my plane was the last one in before the doors were secured, but stepping down from the Jostens plane, I noticed another aircraft behind mine with a man and woman getting out. The aircraft was a Navion and had a color strip along the side of the aircraft. Upon close examination, I noticed that it was a broken line of Morse code, which spelled out Betty Haas. -.... . - - -.-- .... .- .- ...

Betty was the stewardess I remembered from my time flying with Pan Am. In a conversation with Betty, I learned that she had recently married and her husband was making an effort to learn to fly. After a short visit and clearing skies, I wished them many happy years and departed to finish our circuit. I'd always liked and respected Betty—a talented "airman" if there ever was one.

Flying a Surgeon—and Making Friends

The Mayo hospital had a crucial surgery scheduled for a very important individual. They looked around for the most qualified surgeon and found him in New York. He was urgently summoned to Rochester, Minnesota to perform the operation.

The surgeon was en route from New York on Northwest airlines with a stop scheduled for Chicago O'Hare field and then on to Minneapolis, where he would receive ground transportation down to Rochester.

It was decided to take the surgeon off the Northwest flight at Chicago and fly him directly to Rochester. I was waiting for him with a flashing green light and a card on which I had boldly printed "Mayo." He quickly identified me as his next transport. At that point, a man hurried by in the opposite direction carrying a half-opened brief case. He hollered, "Hiya', Tommy!" The

Hannibal, Missouri: The three Jostens airplanes. The middle one is the Cessna 310 I hand-started in Backus, MN.

surgeon asked, "Who was that?" And I said, "The former Congressman and Governor Al Quie. Whereupon the surgeon asked, "How does he know you?" I replied, "In the same fashion that you'll know me, the next time you see me." We proceeded to get him to Rochester for the urgent operation in good time.

Report of a Fire From the Air

I remember vividly the 6:00 AM takeoff from Rochester International Airport (RST) where, on climb-out about two miles southeast of the airport, I noticed a house with smoke billowing out from under the eaves, but not yet aflame. I radioed back to the Rochester tower to send fire equipment.

With my passenger aboard, I made a tight 360-degree turn, put my props in full low pitch, and flew at full power back across the roof low enough to almost pull the shingles off. Then I circled and looked to see if anyone might come out. My low flyover woke the neighbors but no occupants emerged from the burning home. I talked again with the tower and then resumed my flight to Chicago.

It was still daylight when I made my return flight that evening, so I flew over the site to see the charred remains and asked the tower for news of survivors. I was relieved to hear the house had been unoccupied, with the people on vacation and no pets left at home.

Dogfight Displeases Boss

Under the Naval Reserve program, in order to maintain our flight certification, Bob Crocker, a former Marine pilot, and I flew one of our small aircraft to the Naval Reserve station at the MSP (Minneapolis-St. Paul) airport and obtained two Navy fighter planes. Then we flew back to Owatonna and, directly over the town, engaged in aerial acrobatics and a simulated dogfight for 20 minutes or so. Soon, a crowd had gathered to watch, many leaving their places of employment to do so. Walter Gainey came out to the local airport on our return to complain that a large portion of the Jostens

Jostens Cessna Citation at Fremont, Nebraska.

workers had left their workstations and gone outside to observe the aerial show.

A Celebrity Tragedy

On March 23, 1958, I was flying Dan C. Gainey to Scottsdale, Arizona, in a Cessna 310. I passed directly over the crash site of a Lockheed Lodestar that had occurred the previous day. It turned out to be the accident that killed Mike Todd, the former husband of actress Elizabeth Taylor.

Delivering Peaches for Dan C. Gainey

I spent a good deal of my time in the air for Jostens flying Dan C. Gainey around the country, for his business and also his pleasure pursuits, such as fishing trips. But every year there was a special mission I flew at Dan C. Gainey's request. In the season when peach crops came ripe in the southern parts of the country, we were blessed by the generosity of Daniel C. Gainey, who had me take the seats out of our twin-engine airplane and fly to wherever the peaches were at their best. That would mean flights to Georgia and sometimes Missouri. On these flights, I would go alone and then drive from the airport to wherever the crop was ripe, right to the farm.

I would seek the most prime ripe peaches and make a deal with the grower, who then packed them into wooden boxes and delivered them to the airport. We packed the plane as full as space would allow, loading the craft carefully to avoid weight imbalance. I would fly the cargo of peaches to Owatonna where Joe Dulak would meet me at the airport. We unloaded them and took them to a Gainey property where they would be packaged in large paper sacks. Following Dan C. Gainey's list, Joe and I drove around and gave the peaches to various happy recipients. I would always bring a bag of peaches home to my family as well.

Tricky Landings and Other Sticky Situations

In my flying days, I had acquired the habit of post-flight critiquing, particularly if I had made a difficult flight, such as any of my instrument landing system (ILS) approaches made in dicey conditions when visibility was limited to none. I came to the conclusion that air traffic controllers erred on the side of keeping airports open when conditions were below the minimums, calling it "200 and a quarter mile" and thus testing limits of pilots and equipment. A wintry Learjet landing on an icy runway at Washington Dulles at minimums was one to be satisfied with in post-flight critique. I was copilot in the Learjet, and we were cleared for an approach into Dulles. But then the pilot refused. He said he couldn't make the landing himself because he was afraid that, because of the ice, he would not be able to control the airplane once on the ground. He just looked at me and said, "I can't do it—you've got it." Recognizing that he had far less flying experience than me, I took over and landed the plane safely.

Precision Approach

An earlier landing in Minneapolis, in a Beechcraft twin engine Bonanza, is etched in my memory. It was early evening on Christmas Eve, and I had started out from Oklahoma City, Oklahoma, in good visual conditions, with a flight plan destination of Owatonna, Minnesota. When passing Des Moines, Iowa, it appeared that the weather ahead was deteriorating rapidly with snow, low ceilings and icing conditions. Those things meant that landing in Owatonna was out of the question. By the time I reached Mason City, Iowa, I was in radio contact with Minneapolis control, and flying between layers. I was notified that Minneapolis was at minimums and approach control vectored me to fit into a sequence of airline flights inbound to Minneapolis. Using an instrument landing approach I was directed to runway 4 and asked to keep my speed up to near cruising until I reached the outer marker in order to accommodate other aircraft.

By that time, I recognized that this had to be a precision approach, that I had no other choice of going elsewhere if I couldn't find the runway. I had a United Airlines plane ahead and a North Central behind me asking, "Where's that little plane now?" When the United flight radioed saying they couldn't find the runway and were executing the missed-approach procedure, the tower gave them clearance to climb and a heading to fly. He called back immediately with the complaint about being vectored into a thunderhead. The tower gave him another route, and I thought, "Wow, radar-equipped airliner, thunderstorm, icing, below minimums...I'd better not mess up this one." In heavy snow and light icing, I reported seeing the outer marker and was cleared for landing. I had up-to-the-minute altimeter settings and continued my descent on the localizer to 200 feet and beyond the middle marker, well below that, until those beautiful sequenced high-intensity approach lights (like tracer bullets) led me down to the runway.

When I was about to touch down, the North Central radioed again asking, "Where's that little airplane?" The tower responded, "He's on the ground, now let's see what you can do." I parked the plane and called the tower to thank them for—as they say in Motel 6 advertisements—"keeping the lights on for me." They said the airport had just closed, and that I was among the last to get in. I wished them a Merry Christmas and rented a car for the drive home.

For a Pilot, Judgment Matters

On a summer afternoon I flew a Cessna 310 twin-engine for Jostens from Owatonna with one passenger to Backus in northern Minnesota. The airport there was unattended, no hangars, no parked airplanes, no people, no service, nothing but a windsock and mowed grass strip for landing.

There was a car and driver to meet our arrival. After baggage transfer, the driver asked if I needed anything, then drove off and out of sight. I got back in my plane for the second leg of the flight plan: alone to Chicago, to pick up two, fly return to Owatonna. But surprise! I couldn't get even a click in my attempts to start either engine. Apparently our newly-installed, nickel-cadmium batteries had completely discharged at shutdown.

With no phone or help in sight, I walked about a half mile down a tree-lined gravel road to an intersection with what in flight had looked like a gas station. It turned out to be just a small country store with long-ago shut-down fuel pump, no phone, and a lone old woman in charge. I told her of my plight and asked her to send any man or boys who might come by to assist at the airstrip.

Back at the plane. I decided to try to start the engine myself. I set the brakes, rolled a big stone in front of the right main wheel, pulled the propeller through compression position, and hopped in the plane. Back at the controls, I turned the ignition switch to ON, opened the right engine throttle a bit, and tightened the friction knob on the throttle to avoid a runaway advance of power if the engine should start.

Then back out front, checked for firm footing, and—keeping in mind my retreat path—I reached high and pulled down firmly on the propeller. The engine sprang to life as I leapt away and back inside to stabilize the power; then back out front of the plane to remove the big stone; returning to easily start the other engine, went through preflight checklists, and took off for Chicago. One would very rarely see that starting

Jostens Learjet that I flew, June 1968.

procedure on such an aircraft even in the late 1950s—and never by a lone pilot.

In Chicago I landed, picked up my passengers, and the plane ran fine after that. One thing about those single-wing, twin-engine airplanes: When you "prop it" (start by hand as I did), you are standing right where the propellers are spinning. Like so much about flying, make one bad judgment as a pilot and you are a dead man.

Green Bay Packers and a Jostens Sales Rep

Jostens' sales reps often pursued people prominent in the fields of education and sports, knowing their association with our company would be good for sales. During my tenure as Chief Pilot, I noted a strong relationship with the Green Bay Packers. Awakened at home after midnight on a very cold night in January many years ago, I was made aware of a problem. A plane had been chartered to fly Bart Starr and three others back home to Green Bay after an all-day promotion in Owatonna. Their plane, an Aero Commander, had been outside all day in sub-zero temperatures. An engine start was extremely unlikely.

Thinking that as a backup plan, I might be asked to make the flight in Jostens' equipment, I checked with Rochester Weather. I was told icing, snow, low ceilings, and low visibility in the Milwaukee/Green Bay area were predicted! I made the decision that the flight was not for my skills or equipment. Wondering about their charter pilot and his aircraft, I loaded up some cold-start gear and went across the field to offer my assistance. After considerable effort, I started one engine, but had no luck with the other. A look at the chartered plane's logbooks and some talk with the pilot convinced me that even with both engines warmed up, neither the charter pilot nor the airplane were up to the planned trip under the poor conditions. We both conveyed that conclusion through the Jostens executives to the Packers group. The Packers were sent back to their motel in Owatonna having given orders to send a better airplane and crew for the flight home the next day.

Tom Walsh stands next to the tail of the Jostens Learjet. Mr. Gainey assigned the 24KT on the tail to stand for "Twenty-Four Karat."

Helping a Nun in Need

Charlie Oswald, another Jostens executive, instructed me to fly to the Hutchinson, Kansas Airport (HUT) on a "mission of mercy." Oswald's wife's sister was hospitalized at the Mayo facility in Rochester, where she was known to be dying of cancer. The ailing sister's dear friend was a Catholic nun living in Hutchison. It was winter, and icy weather conditions threatened our plans. However, I was able to complete the flight under Instrument Flight Rules (IFC), landing at Rochester, Minnesota (RST) as planned. The nun was able to be at her friend's bedside.

Famous People

During my time at Jostens, I flew other notable people, including preeminent Catholic clergy, Governors and Congressmen, even future president Gerald Ford (then Speaker of the House of Representatives). The Ford flight was from Fargo, North Dakota to Mankato, Minnesota and required no security. It was just the two of us in the front of our Beechcraft Bonanza. The weather was fine, and I enjoyed a pleasant hour or so with the future president.

"Presented to Thomas Walsh in recognition and appreciation for the more than 2,000,000 miles safely flown as Chief Pilot for Josten's, Inc. [Signed] Dan C. Gainey, Chairman, Dan J. Gainey, President, March 8, 1968"

"This Is My Pilot"

Once a Navy man, always a Navy man. At the Republican convention in Chicago in 1968, Dan C. Gainey, who was the treasurer of the party, hosted a reception at the Sheraton Blackstone Hotel.

President Dwight D. "Ike" Eisenhower was the honored guest. On his arrival in the ballroom, Ike and Dan stood in the middle of the ballroom as music played softly. After a few moments, Dan looked over at the table where I was seated with his son. He motioned with a finger wave to join him. I tapped his son on the arm and said, "Your dad wants you out there." After a brief glance at his father, he replied, "No, he wants you."

After that I stood up and buttoned my jacket and proceeded to join Dan and Ike. By way of introduction, the boss said, "This is my pilot." Ike responded, saying "Yes, but he probably also flew for me."

I nodded and told him that I had been a fighter pilot in the Navy in World War II. After a few more remarks, I returned to my table, thinking what a high honor it had been to be asked to join these two leaders. As so often happens, what I really wanted to say didn't occur to me until I was back in my seat. I wish that I had found it convenient to mention my younger brother Raymond, who had earned the Distinguished Flying Cross after he shot down a German buzz bomb.

Summer 1946 Cashman Field, Owatonna. Tom Walsh greeting Joe Foss, WWII USMC Ace South Pacific and soon to become governor of South Dakota. Photo by Steele County Photo News Co. Owatonna, Minnesota.

More Government Officials

I also flew Congressman/Governor Albert Quie on multiple occasions. I took an American Airlines flight from New York to Washington to deliver a gift to Vice President Nixon's residence and met Nixon's gracious wife, Pat, at the back door. I returned to New York on an American Airlines Convair with then-Senator John F. Kennedy.

I greeted Joe Foss, U.S. Marine Corps, World War II Ace, and Governor of South Dakota when he flew into Owatonna's early airport, Cashman Field in 1946.

1970: It Was Leaving Time—Again

Matters at Jostens grew complicated due to differences between Charlie Oswald and Dan C. Gainey over corporate strategy. When Oswald was hired, he was one of several recent graduates of Harvard Business School that Jostens had been encouraged to employ as part of a plan to take the company into public ownership and membership in the New York Stock Exchange. Oswald did achieve this prestigious listing for the company, and was named Corporate Comptroller. But over time, Oswald and Gainey remained in frequent opposition over corporate developments.

As the company's pilot, I was in a position to observe and overhear inside information whether I wanted to or not. At times, this became awkward. I was a conduit of information to Gainey, which displeased Oswald. This opposition caused Oswald to put obstacles in my way when he could.

On one occasion, I learned Oswald was building a block within the board of directors to act as an investment group exclusively under his control. He was mounting a serious effort to achieve ownership of companies in the school jewelry business. While flying this investment team to Chicago, I overheard a conversation en route about an expected corporate acquisition. A 3-million-dollar commission was at stake. I asked

Speed Records

- Owatonna to New York City to the LaGuardia Airport (LGA) nonstop in Bonanza N5424D in five hours and twenty minutes.
- Jostens Learjet from Santa Barbara, California to Owatonna, Minnesota in two hours and forty-five minutes.

permission to join this group, but Oswald denied my request.

On another occasion, Dan C. Gainey asked me to fly him and his son Dan J. to Denver, Colorado for a trout-fishing trip. They were attired and equipped for such an endeavor. I dropped them at the Denver airport, where the boss said, "I'll call you in a couple of days when we want you to come back and pick us up." He assumed I would return promptly to Owatonna, which I had planned to do. However, my departure was delayed due to a minor radio problem soon fixed with the help of skilled technicians at the Denver airport.

While they worked, I tidied up the cabin area. Someone had left a copy of the latest Wall Street Journal stock reports, which I picked up. Boldly encircled was the price of Jostens and also Boise Cascade. This immediately rang a bell in my mind. I looked down the line of corporate jet aircraft and noted one way down on the end with the identification mark on the tail: BC for Boise Cascade. Suddenly Dan C. Gainey reappeared and said, “Why aren’t you halfway back to Owatonna by now?” I reported the radio malfunction. Dan asked, “Are you aware of what is going on?” I silently nodded, yes. Then Dan asked about my copilot. I said, “No, he doesn’t have the faintest idea,” whereupon Dan said, “Keep it that way.”

I flew back to Owatonna early that afternoon. Walking down “mahogany row” (as we called the corporate executives’ offices), I ran into Charles Oswald, who asked where I had been. I told him of the trip to Denver with Dan and his son. Oswald smilingly asked if I had any questions. I replied, “Which stock purchase would be profitable?” Oswald remarked, “You cannot be involved, you are an insider now.” Then he added, “But don’t be concerned. It’s not going to work, In fact, it’s failed already.” I related this exchange to Dan C. Gainey, who was, after all, Oswald’s boss.

As these two stories show, there was a general sense of turmoil in corporate management at Jostens. This corporate struggle for control reached a point one day where Dan C. Gainey said to me, “Get me a gun. I am going to kill somebody!” My response was, “No, we’ll succeed.” And we did.

Eventually, Dan asked me to take on mentoring his son, shifting me from Chief Pilot to a corporate role as assistant to the young man. He had an admiration for my forthrightness, which he had witnessed on occasions when I disagreed with air traffic controllers.

Dan C. wanted Dan J. to follow him in leadership at Jostens, but judged him to be lacking the aggressive temperament needed. He thought some of my fighting spirit and competitiveness might help the young man succeed. I did what I could to help father and son, while trying to stay out of the conflict in the corporation. Dan J. did rise to the office of president, while his father, Dan C., served as chairman of the board. In time, this internal strife led to my retirement. On June 30, 1970, my Jostens employment officially ended after 16 years, 8 months, 10 days.

Part of the retirement package I negotiated enabled me to buy one of Jostens' planes. In addition to a Beechcraft Bonanza, I purchased a hangar. I was certified by the FAA and the Bureau of Aeronautics of Minnesota for air taxi operations. I enjoyed that activity for several years, flying people and small cargo to places and in situations not suitable for commercial airlines. Before long I would be involved in more business ventures in Owatonna.

Chapter 8: Business Pursuits 1970–1990s

Owatonna at the time I moved there in 1953 was a pleasant little town on the Minnesota prairies, situated about halfway between Minneapolis–St. Paul and Rochester and home to the world-famous Mayo Clinic. Even though Owatonna was small in size, it was big in impact: a number of successful companies had gotten their start, and still thrive, there. With so much industrial activity, my Navy buddy, Glenn Degner, had been right to believe his hometown needed an airport, back at the end of World War II. I had also found a good friend in Terry Cashman, part of a large family in town, who had been involved with our startup of the Owatonna airport operation.

With my busy flying schedule, I was away from Owatonna too much to be very involved in community service, but I did volunteer when I could. During the polio epidemic I headed up the retail coin collection for the Steele County March of Dimes program. Later I served for nine years as a member and chairman of the Municipal Airport Commission and for 25 years as a member of the board of directors of the Owatonna State Bank. By the time I retired in the 1990s, Owatonna was larger, but still a close-knit community.

While at Jostens, Other Business Pursuits

While flying for Jostens, I continued to be involved with the Owatonna airport I had helped start with Glenn Degner and Joe Dulak. We operated a business called SOMINA, or Southern Minnesota Aviation, which had started operations at the temporary airport in Owatonna even before the commercial airport opened there.

Then I branched out—first in real estate, a field I was already familiar with, and then into other lines of business.

Northstar: Our Family of Companies

Early on in organizing my business affairs, I was advised to establish a corporation that would be an umbrella for our various businesses. On January 3, 1963 I founded Northstar, Incorporated, with the help of my attorneys, the Walbran Law Firm. We registered as a Minnesota corporation with my wife, Martha, and myself as its sole stockholders.

I chose as a logo the outline of the state of Minnesota, with a star located approximately in the Owatonna area. I did not copyright that logo, and it appeared that later on it was picked up by the local chamber of commerce and other state organizations.

Under the Northstar Inc. parent company we registered the name Northstar Realty with the County Clerk. Our immediate intent for the company was to improve how we managed our growing real estate interests. We owned some 37 apartment units and several commercial properties by that time. Northstar Realty became a collection of properties purchased for rehab and further sale. Later, I established another business, Northstar Travel Service.

Northstar Realty

Art Olson, a popular candidate for County Judge, recommended I get a real estate license and start buying available properties. He sent appraisal jobs my way. Northstar Realty offered sales, property management, and appraisals. It grew over time, and I later hired a couple of salesmen.

At one time during that period, I was asked to testify as to land value in an action against the State of Minnesota. The state's attorney questioned my credentials as an expert witness, saying, "You are just a pilot." I wanted to respond, "I have already viewed more real estate then you will in your entire life," but our attorney dissuaded me, saying that the jury would make the judgment in that regard. They did—with a generous award for our side.

Landlord Woes

Being a real estate owner makes one a landlord, and with that role comes any number of problems. Sometimes, I thought I was back on the police beat.

One Sunday, as I was getting ready to go to church, I received a call from a tenant who said that her toilet was running over onto the floor. I told her, "Quit flushing, then." She did, but I drove over to have a look at the situation. I took my jacket off and rolled up a sleeve.

She said, "You're not going to put your hand in there, are you?"

I said, "Yes, I am." I reached down into the mess and was able to pull out a pile of tissue and beyond it, a toothbrush. Then the water flushed as it should, and the toilet functioned properly again.

Problems with slow-pay or no-pay tenants were not unusual. I had one tenant who was a couple months behind in payments, and he would say next week he would have the money. This did not make him popular with me, nor did the fact that he had three cats. Well, it got to the point where, in order to get his attention, I addressed a note to the three cats. I told them that they were going to have to find a new home because their master was not paying the rent. If they would like to stay there, they would have to get him to pay up on time. That actually worked!

There was another tenant, a woman, who had several cats, too. She was a high school principal. Various tenants who had children organized together to use the principal's apartment as the place where they would take turns babysitting each other's children, including the principal's kids. Eventually they all agreed the apartment was too unpleasant due to the cats soiling the carpets. They reported this to me. I then told the principal that she and her family had to leave. I faced quite a job to eliminate the odor, which meant tearing up the carpet and cleaning the apartment. I required the principal to reimburse me for several hundred dollars in expenses.

Another tenant problem I recall involved a couple of young men who rented a ground floor apartment. When they moved their Harley-Davidson motorcycle into the living room to overhaul the engine, I was forced to ask them to move. Shortly after, there was a fire in the furnace room of the building, rolled-up newspapers and such set on fire. It was detected soon after it first started, and a neighbor was able to get it under control before the fire engines arrived. It was never proven—but I strongly suspect—that the motorcycle boys had created this problem as revenge for being evicted. However, I could not prove it.

Real Estate Investments

My initial real estate purchases included two houses on Rose Street in Owatonna; one became our family home and I had the other converted into a duplex. This was the start of many rental properties. These were purchased with money I had saved during wartime service in the Navy along with a mortgage from Owatonna Savings and Loan.

Shortly after these purchases, I became aware of a family home across the street that was slated for sale by the sheriff to satisfy a real estate tax delinquency. My father-in-law assisted me in purchasing that property at auction.

The bidding took place on the county court house steps. Each time I made a bid, there was a woman who responded with an increase of 25 cents. Finally, the sheriff lost patience with this and gave me the opportunity to buy the property for a modest sum. I converted it to a duplex and found a two-car garage for sale and had house movers move it to the site.

Later, I purchased a one-family house farther east on Rose Street. I moved it to a lot a few doors up the street, which made an adjacent lot plus the original lot sufficient space to accommodate a 12-unit apartment building. This I had built, and added it to the previously held rental properties owned by Northstar Realty. As realtors at that time we also sold numerous properties for Daniel C. Gainey, which included supermarkets in four locations in Minnesota and Wisconsin.

Northstar Realty purchased one of these—a Piggly Wiggly property in Owatonna. The grocery store was adjacent to a large old house on Pearl Street. I purchased that house and demolished it in order to use the site to build a concrete block, three-story, 15-unit apartment building, with the ground floor developed for commercial office tenants. Just prior to this purchase, I had bought the Degner travel agency. I had plans to situate the travel agency, the latest of my Northstar businesses, in my new building. I also moved our Northstar Realty sales office out to the new Pearl Street building.

Northstar Aviation

When I retired from Jostens, I started Northstar Aviation with the Beechcraft Bonanza and hangar I purchased from Jostens. Flying afforded occasions to meet and serve many famous people, among them former Congressman/Governor Al Quie, former President Gerald Ford. Once I was even briefly introduced to, and had a brief conversation with, then President, Dwight Eisenhower.

Tired of Landing & Departure Delays

FLY THERE!

FAST, CONVENIENT TRANSPORTATION TO OUT OF THE WAY PLACES.

RELIABLE, INSURED, EXPERIENCED.

TOM WALSH

NORTHSTAR AVIATION

Call 451-1640 or 451-3684

A flyer advertising Northstar Aviation.

My Beechcraft Bonanza instrument panel.

H35 Serial D4928, Beechcraft Bonanza owned by Tom Walsh, Northstar Aviation.

Tom Walsh about 1970, about the time I was starting Northstar.

Stories from Northstar Aviation

As the pilot and head of an aviation service, I had any number of interesting encounters. Several stand out in memory.

On the Road to Jericho

The road to Jericho was the setting for the parable of the Good Samaritan, told in the Bible. I had my opportunity to be a good Samaritan on the road near Medford, a town about halfway between Minneapolis-St. Paul and Owatonna. Back in the late 1970s on an August afternoon, there was a single vehicle accident in the southbound lanes of I-35 near Medford. The car was a total loss, but the people in it were uninjured.

The travelers were a priest and two nuns en route from St. Paul to their home base in Missouri. The trooper responding to the scene assisted in the arrangements to remove the disabled car, and took them and their baggage to the Owatonna airport thinking there was a travel agency with a car rental franchise there. We had purchased and removed that service some years before, but a call to downtown brought me quickly to the airport to explain that my Northstar Travel Service Avis franchise had no "floater" cars to send to destinations other than Minneapolis or Rochester, and that I could rent them a car to MSP to put them back at "square one." But then I had a better idea, saying, "See that small hangar across the field? There's a fully fueled airplane inside. I'm the pilot. The weather's fine and I can have you home before dark." The priest responded that would be great but far too costly for them. I told him that they'd had misfortune enough and that I was there somehow to help with the rest of their day.

With a few phone calls for the flight plan and home and with the trooper's blessings, we were off for our pleasant two-hour-and-twenty-minute flight. I radioed ahead for our sundown arrival, and had a warm reception. I was offered meals and overnight accommodations which I declined. They somehow arranged to pay for the fuel it took to refill for the flight home.

One of the nuns wondered, "Isn't it scary to fly all alone up there in the dark of night?"

I told her, "That's the glory of it. I'm sure I'll be supported tonight by your prayers."

Blessings

The following anecdote comes from a congratulatory message I sent to my friend, Linda Clader, a former professor of classical literature at Carleton College on the occasion of her ordination to the priesthood at St. Paul's Episcopal Church in Owatonna.

Several years ago while operating my charter flying venture, I flew several people into the old airport at Wausau, Wisconsin and agreed to remain at the airport until their return for the trip back home. After their departure on a business errand, I walked to the flight shack to see about refueling my airplane.

At a desk there was an old pilot of my vintage sprawled out in a relaxed manner, a man I had not seen in many years. He was the airport operator, chief pilot, flight instructor, mechanic, and a certified flight examiner. He greeted me with a remark and ended by expressing amazement that "this old SOB was still flying." He then turned toward a bright looking young man he had been talking to and in mild apology said, "I'd better mind my language lest I upset this fellow, he's a young minister and about to take me up for a ride to demonstrate his newfound skills and have me issue his license." With that he dismissed the young man, directing him to go out to his plane and start a preflight examination of the aircraft. I placed my fuel order and started back to my plane to tidy up its interior and find some reading material. On the way I had to pass the plane where the young pilot was checking ailerons, empennage and pitot—respectively, the moving control surfaces on the edge of the wing and tail and an instrument for measuring the plane's speed. Without any deliberate thought or intent, I walked up to him, took both of his hands in mine, exchanged smiles, and without a word turned and left him with a puzzled look on his face.

Back on the flight line after an hour or two, I recognized the young minister again preparing to depart. I approached and asked the outcome of his flight check. His face just lit up with the brightest of smiles as he said that he had passed and that he was looking forward to using this new skill in the service of mankind for the Lord. Then he looked at me more directly and asked about the meaning of my wordless gesture to him earlier. I paused and after brief reflection told him that it represented the passing on of more than 35 years of safe flying, thousands of hours in worldwide places and circumstances, that it was a precious gift, residing in my hands or my eyes or somewhere within, and that I wanted to share it with him. I told him that I felt somewhat uneasy about my spontaneous gesture, that in essence it represented a reversal of roles, it perhaps being more appropriate for him to place a benediction on me than me on him. He graciously dismissed that thought saying he was so grateful for that moment and would treasure the memory all the days of his life. We spoke briefly, sincerely wished each other well, and parted.

Attending Linda's ordination was a somewhat similar situation, except that I had more of a feeling of unworthiness. I would reverse our roles, smile, take Linda's hands in mine, and try to share the manifold blessings I have enjoyed during my long life.

"Blessed are the pure in heart for they shall see God." – *Matthew 5:8*

Family Changes

There were changes on the family front during the 1960s: My daughter Holly Ann (Holly) was born on Christmas Day, 1963 in St. Mary's Hospital in Rochester.

Our youngest became the source of many family stories. When Holly was at her christening, the priest in charge, Monsignor Castle, asked, "What will the child's name be?"

I said, "Holly."

He said, "Oh, no, she is not holy yet. Not until I finish with her."

On her third birthday, she received as a Christmas present a pair of child's starter skates—double blades on each foot. We were down on the river on our skating rink and along came our neighbor and friend, Kay Tilletson. Kay asked Holly how old she was. Holly held up her hand, then said, "I can't tell you. I have my mittens on."

And we'll never forget, Saturday, August 12, 1967. We were living at 222 East School Street at the time. After coming home from playing golf, I was in the downstairs lavatory washing my hands at the sink, with my folding golf cart right behind me. Holly came in and, before I could notice, she put her finger into a metal-hinged folding seat on the golf cart. When I sat down, it somehow closed that hinge, which nipped off the tip of her finger. I seized her hand and put it under the faucet to wash away the rapid flow of blood, and called to son Dan to find that missing portion of her finger. We called Dr. Ted Stransky, our family doctor, and said that we would meet him at the emergency area in the hospital with temporary bandage and applying pressure along the way. Trying to reduce the flow of blood with pressure on the injured limb, we took Holly to the hospital where we met our doctor. He proceeded to sew the missing fingertip back where it belonged. As I watched, the doctor took a look at me, suddenly barking, "Get him out of here!" I must have appeared pale and about to lose consciousness. Somehow, watching my daughter was more stressful than even the many gruesome situations I had experienced in my work as a cop.

Other changes were that Martha and I sold our School Street house and moved to our 140 West Pearl Street residence.

In 1967 I turned 50 years old and began to need some medical maintenance myself. I had total replacement surgery on my left hip at Mayo Methodist in August, 1968. We're both grateful to the excellent medical care available in Rochester just 40 miles away. I would have my other hip replaced in 1977, more hip surgeries in 1979 and 1982, and a final hip replacement in 1996 (age 77).

My eyes began to need attention as well. In 1987 I underwent eye surgery for cataract removal from my left eye and an intraocular lens implant. In 1989 I had another eye surgery using laser technology, which was brand new at the time.

More Business Ventures

My business pursuits in the 1960s and '70s brought more opportunities my way. Among them: I was involved in bringing a bank to Owatonna and purchased a travel company to expand the operations of Northstar Aviation.

Owatonna State Bank

As I became more involved in the business community of Owatonna, I saw the merit in Owatonna's having its own bank though to do so it would have to attract a rural bank charter. This became Oakdale State Bank (now known as United Prairie Bank of Owatonna). I served as a director on its board for 25 years.

This had little to do with aviation, except for the occasional aerial photo ops and inspections of rural properties and mortgaged machinery. It was convenient that I was a licensed pilot with my beloved Bonanza available for our flights.

In 1960, a property that I listed for sale included a former laundry and dry-cleaning business, which had drive-up access. I recall sitting on the steps of another property I had listed that was across the street, chatting with the owner, Karl Dahlstrom. We speculated about different possible uses of that drive-up business. I suggested a drive-in bank, since the building already had a big steel vault and modern drive-in access. Karl said that might be difficult, but could possibly be done by moving one or two small bank charters to Owatonna from neighboring communities.

With that in mind, my next challenge was to find a rural bank willing to move to this location. I was directed to Pierce Jones, whose bank charters in Medford and Meriden, Minnesota might be eligible for consideration. Pierce, whom everyone called "Pop" Jones, was a legendary country banker, an outspoken man who could really hold forth on traditional banking customs and procedures. There was a lot of opposition to our effort from the local banks. We appealed to the state banking authorities to move the bank charter from Medford to Owatonna. After great effort, and a little compromise, our efforts succeeded. We were authorized to move not the Medford but the Meriden bank charter to town.

Pop Jones wanted to bring his son, Ferris Jones, into this idea. His son had recently lost his wife and was courting the daughter of Karl Dahlstrom, the very man I was sitting with when the idea of bringing a bank to Owatonna occurred to me. The courtship was short and successful in that Ferris married the daughter (known by the nickname Dolly), and they went on a honeymoon to Las Vegas. They returned from there to step into the new Oakdale State Bank.

On February 3, 1961, the Oakdale State Bank opened for business. Harold Edmond and I were elected to the board of directors.

We purchased the property, which was located just south of the fairgrounds, and financed and erected a new modern bank building. Later, due to conflict with a bank of a similar name in St. Paul, it was renamed the Owatonna State Bank.

With the purchase of token shares of stock, I was elected to the bank's Board of Directors, serving in that capacity through three changes of ownership over the next 25 years.

Northstar Travel Service

On July 1, 1974 our company, Northstar, Inc. purchased Degner Travel Service. We renamed it Northstar Travel Service and moved the operation from the Owatonna

A group of new Northstar travel agents at a Pan Am training session in New York City 1974. Martha and I are at the far right.

Airport to a rental location. In 1978, soon after of the apartment building at 140 W. Pearl Street was completed, we moved Northstar Travel Service to the ground floor. We also leased space to Bishman/Schuette Insurance there.

Northstar Travel Service grew to the point where we opened a branch operation in Waseca. During this period, I was a member of the Association of Independent Travel Agents and served for a year as the association's president. My wife, Martha, managed the travel office.

Being part of the "family" in a family-owned businesses isn't always easy, and neither is managing a mix of family members and employees. One day at

THIS TRAVEL AGENT IS

. . . a citizen of the United States . . . a U.S. Navy veteran . . . a four gallon plus donor to the Red Cross Blood Program . . . supports principles of the free enterprise system by word, association and donations . . . a past and ongoing contributor to United Fund and to most of many dedicated appeals of hospitals, medical research, charitable and welfare organizations and various churches, political candidates, student activities and individual pleas for help . . . has served on boards, committees in community service organizations for many years . . . a 20,000 hour pilot with in depth experience with the airlines, military, police and corporate areas of aviation . . . around the world and all 50 United States . . . presently satisfying some very discriminating patronage . . . and asking your consideration for the service we can provide and which you deserve.

. . . a member of the American Society of Travel Agents.

WILL
- Save you time
- Qualify you for least expensive fares
- Accept major credit cards

GUARANTEE — the best of **SERVICE** in the use of our experienced staff and ultra-modern computer equipment.

DIVISION OF NORTH STAR INC.
Box 511 • Owatonna, Minn. 55060
(507) 451-5600

A GOOD TRAVEL AGENT CAN . . .

. . . help you far beyond an ordinary ticket seller. He or she is a specialist with the experience and ability to show you how to travel the best way — within your budget.

When you use a travel agent, you get a lot of extras you don't have to pay for. Because commissions are the main source of the travel agent's income.

For example, a travel agent arranging your transportation gets a commission from the airline. The cost to you? Exactly the same you'd pay at the airline counter.

In most cases, hotel reservations are often made without charge to you, when it's covered by the travel agent's commission. If not, there's only a nominal charge to cover telephone calls or other correspondence needed to make your reservations.

In the exciting world of travel, your travel agent is the authority. It's the travel agent's business to intimately know the places to go. How to get there. Where to stay. All for your travelling pleasure and comfort.

Sure, planning your own trip is fun. But arranging its details isn't. Telephone calls. Hotel correspondence. Transportation connections. That's your travel agent's business. Also, it's another way he or she can save you money.

Your travel agent has the latest information on rates and schedules, inclusive tours and charters. Your travel agent has established connections, worldwide. All to give you a neat package of tickets, coupons, and reservations. And faster than anyone.

It's the right way to begin any trip you'd like to remember always.

So once you've decided to go anywhere, begin with your local travel agent. You'll get helpful advice on flight schedules and fares, inclusive tours and charters, hotels, restaurants, sightseeing, and shopping. Then when your itinerary is final, your travel agent will bring everything together for you — for a pleasant and memorable trip.

We can send you to Orlando via MARS.

It's not the long way to go. It's the instant way to know when you're going. And it's the most reliable. Because with MARSPLUS service we now have the capability to connect directly into the computer of every airline on our system. That means we know what they know. And that's the plus for you.

So wherever you want to go, whether it's Florida, the Big Apple, or the Land of the Rising Sun, we can send you via MARS, our multi-access reservation system. MARSPLUS, the ultimate reservation service from ITT.

Come on in today, or call us. We'll show you what it's like to travel via MARS.

MARSPLUS™
Reservations via ITT Electronic Travel Services

CREDIT CARDS ARE WELCOME HERE

Credit cards postpone
Your payment due dates

Fine with us!

Good for you!
CASH FLOW SITUATION.
Good for ours, too.

Airlines give us some bad
Cash Flow problems

Travel agents must
Pay for all tickets issued
Within a 5 day average.

That is rough going when
Companies ask us for
15 and 30 day credit.

Sure, we will cooperate
With you . . .
As long as our
Receivables don't
Skyrocket out of sight!

Let's work it out so
We both find
Financing no sweat.
Thanks!

Front and back of a brochure advertising Northstar Travel Service.

noontime Martha departed for lunch. Just before that, I had noted that our four telephone lines were on hold. Looking around at the office workstations, I could not see anybody appearing to have a telephone connection on hold. Then, the four gals we employed as travel agents approached me together. With one acting as spokesperson for the group, they said I was to remove my wife from our travel agent operation or else they would all quit. I told them immediately that Martha had equal status to me in our corporate structure, and that I could not fire her any more than she could fire me. I observed that, this being the case, I would accept their immediate resignations. They could go to lunch, and I would have their checks available for them upon their return. They were insistent in that demand, and so, in their absence I made out their termination payments with instructions as to how they might apply for unemployment insurance.

All four of these employees transferred their allegiance to a competitive agency, taking with them some much-valued customers. We were grateful for the assistance of our airline supervisor, Jack May, the regional commander for Northwest Airlines, who sent one of his expert agents from Rochester to get us through the week, so we could rehire and continue operation of our agency.

Travels and Adventures

Being in the travel business afforded me and my family opportunities to travel by air and cruise ship to places not seen before: more of Europe, islands in the Caribbean, Central and South America, the Panama Canal, Hawaii, westward across the Pacific several times to Taiwan, Japan, Hong Kong, and inland China, and several spots in Alaska including Kotzebue above the Arctic Circle. I enjoy recalling those trips, including some special memories.

Mont-Saint-Michel Abbey

I was part of a group of about 30 travel agency people making a visit to the Catholic shrine at the abbey of Mont-Saint-Michel on the North Atlantic side of France. The abbey and village are situated on an island accessible by a causeway only at low tide, when trucks and buses and other vehicles can make the short transit. When high tide arrives, the access is completely submerged. The difference between high and low tides is about twelve feet.

I was up at the head of our group, which was crossing the hard-packed sand and starting up the hill. Alongside me was Dale Torgerson, an Owatonnan known for his singing voice. At this time he was moving in on our travel agency business, competing quite aggressively.

He and his wife were unique characters. At the back of the group someone asked Suzy Torgerson, where her husband was. She, with the knowledge that he was up front with the lead group, called out in a loud voice. "Hey, shithead!" That got his attention— along with that of the shocked group.

A Souvenir Lost and Found

My prized cane was purchased in China on one of those trips. In late March and early April 1982, Martha and I took a Northwest Airlines (NWA) flight to Hong Kong and continued on into China. While on this trip, my right hip, which had been replaced with titanium in 1968, started to become problematic. I wandered into a store and saw a cane with a carved dragon on the upper stem. I purchased it for roughly $10.

We had an assisted return on NWA, RONed (that's aviation-code for "remained overnight") at Mary Pat's in Long Beach, California and returned to Minnesota.

I used that dragon cane for the next three decades. Then, on November 5, 2012—30 years later—I lost it. By that time, I was using an electric scooter to get around. As usual, I secured my cane to the scooter with strips of plumber's tape. I had felt the scooter hit a bump but didn't realize that the cane dropped off. After I had travelled several blocks, I realized what had happened and went back to look for it. However, it was nowhere to be found. I did have my contact information on the cane, and I hoped I would see it again, but grew concerned as the days passed.

I placed the following ad in the Owatonna People's Press.

On November 20, reporter Derek Sullivan saw fit to boost my small ad with an article, titled "Resident loses prized cane on trip across town." It explained that I planned on giving the cane to one of my children, with hope that it would become a family heirloom. The article went on to describe my military and aviation career, I suppose to increase readers' sympathy that I deserved to be reunited with my cane.

115 Lost/Found:

LOST CANE
On 22nd St. SE between Federated offices and Hartle Ave. on Monday evening 11/5/12. Dropped from cart to pavement not missed until home arrival and unfound by search soon after. Cane has rounded handle dragon carving on upper stem and owner infro. there too. Family heirloom missed by impaired senior. Reward for information Please call Tom Walsh 413-2595 or 451-1640.

LOST CANE
On 22nd St. SE between Federated offices and Hartle Ave. on Monday evening 11/5/12. Dropped from cart to pavement not missed until home arrival and unfound by search soon after. Cane has rounded handle dragon carving on upper stem and owner info there to. Family heirloom missed by impaired senior. Reward for information. Please call Tom Walsh 413-2595 or 451-1640.

And indeed I was! It was found by someone walking for his health along the route I'd traveled. He saw the ad and article, returned the cane, and asked no reward. The dragon cane is ready to become a family heirloom, just as I had hoped.

Other Travels

In 1978, Martha and I traveled to Greece thanks to the Association of Independent Travel Agents—the trip was a reward for booking a number of trips. Of the destinations offered, we chose Athens, Greece. My daughter lived in California at the time, and her birthday would come while we were in Athens. On that day I tried to get through to her by telephone with a birthday greeting. However, I had no luck making a connection. I got up early the next morning and tried the call again. This time I got through.

"What time is it there?" I asked.

She replied, "Late evening."

"This birthday greeting has arrived on time, then!" I said. She asked what time it was in Greece. I answered, "early morning!"

She replied, "You're up mighty early!"

Because Athens is 10 hours ahead of California, I succeeded in calling her on her birthday—which illustrated the roundness of the world. (This had fascinated me since my trip to Ireland on the SS Westphalia as a little boy.)

On April 20, 1979 we flew to Copenhagen, Denmark. From there we traveled through Stockholm, Sweden then to more southern European countries for a week.

On September 13, 1980 I flew TWA via Chicago and Rome to Athens, Greece. I toured historic places on islands of the Aegean Sea and Mount Olympus and the Corinth Peninsula, where at an ancient amphitheater I was awarded a plaque by the Association of Independent Travel Agents for my year of service as president.

In early May, 1983 Martha and I flew on Koninklijke Luchtvaart Maatschappij (KLM – Royal Dutch Airlines) to Zurich, Switzerland. From there we bussed to Basel, Switzerland and then cruised down the Rhine River on the Brittania, with several overnight stops in France and Germany. We landed in Rotterdam, Netherlands, and spent a few days in and around Amsterdam before flying home.

On March 20, 1984 Martha and I sailed from Fort Lauderdale, Florida on Sun Lines' Stella Solaris to Nassau, Bahamas and the Isle of Madeira. Other stops on this cruise included Spain, Gibraltar, Casablanca, Morocco and Mallorca. We disembarked at Monte Carlo, Monaco to meet and stay a few days with our daughter, Holly, who had a semester abroad from the College of St. Benedict touring Europe. She was based in Aix-en-Provence on the French Riviera. After our visit with Holly, we flew back on a Swissair flight from Nice, France via Zurich, Switzerland and Chicago, Illinois.

On November 29 of that same year, we flew to Hawaii and spent a week on Kauai and then sailed back to San Francisco, California on the American Hawaiian Cruise Line's SS Constitution.

In April, 1992 we flew to England to visit our daughter, Mary Pat, then a major in the U.S. Air Force, living with her family near a Royal Air Force base. We went to London and saw *Miss Saigon*. I enjoyed bowling on the base as well. I noted my scores: 117-106-121-344-116. We flew home LON/MSP nonstop on the great circle route over Greenland and Hudson Bay.

On July 29, 1995, Martha's and my passports expired. At 77, it was time to say *sayonara* and *au revoir* to international travel.

Transition to Retirement

In 1975, I was approaching my 58th birthday when the first of my "retirements" was forced on me, with the loss of my beloved Bonanza. That brought an end to Northstar Aviation, but I continued in my real estate and travel pursuits well into the 1990s.

A Sad End to Northstar Aviation

I will never forget October 2, 1975, the day my single-engine Beechcraft Bonanza caught fire. It was following an emergency landing at the Mankato, Minnesota airport. That pretty much ended my flying activities. I had "wheeled and soared and swung high in the sunlit silence where never lark nor even eagle flew," just as John Gillespie Magee, Jr. wrote in his poem, "High Flight," that I loved so much,

What happened? On a flight to Wyoming, I dropped off two passengers and then with one passenger started the trip back home. Shortly after takeoff, I noticed a strong odor of fuel in the cockpit. The loss of fuel did not seem to be excessive and the engines weren't smoking, with certainly no open flame in the cockpit, so I continued. I maintained a sufficient altitude so I always had a suitable landing place en route, with the thought that if the engine quit I would glide to a landing place at a major airport where there would likely be fire-fighting equipment.

It seemed that the loss of fuel continued at an increasing rate. When we were some miles west of Mankato, I called the Mankato airport and said that due to a fuel loss, I planned to land there. My thinking was that Mankato was served by North Central Airlines and of necessity would have fire and crash equipment on hand.

I kept switching tanks until I got down to the reserve tank. About then the engine quit and I glided to a landing on the active runway.

When the prop stopped windmilling, the passenger said, "Oh, you were not kidding, we didn't have any power there."

I said, "No, that was a forced landing. We had to land somewhere."

The owner-operator sent a fuel truck out to greet us where we were stopped on the runway.

I said, "No, we don't want to refuel here."

I took the passenger back to the terminal area, and after waiting several minutes for more help and perhaps a tow, I tried to start the engine again. I was surprised that the engine got enough fuel to start. I then taxied to the parking area. When going downwind into the parking place, there was enough wind to contain the gas fumes in the engine compartment. The heat of the exhaust touched those fumes off into flame. There was also flame inside the cockpit. I succeeded in putting that out, but I received burns on my legs where my polyester trousers turned to molten plastic.

I vacated the airplane quickly and observed a fuel truck come up again with big extinguishers on the side. The airport workers did not engage them, and the plane

October 2, 1975. My single engine Beechcraft Bonanza in flames.

continued to burn. It did so until the city fire engine came out from Mankato.

I called my wife and said I was going to be late for supper. Then, I called Rochester flight control and cancelled my flight plan. The operator there said, "Aren't you going to fly on to your home base at Owatonna?"

I said, "No, that plane will not be flying again."

The federal crash examiner came the next day and looked at the remains of the aircraft. He had me look at the charred area around the loose fitting where the fire

Burnt Beechcraft Bonanza, October 1975.

Wreckage of Beechcraft Bonanza.

had continued. He said, "That was definitely sabotage. No doubt about it. Do you have any enemies?"

I said, "Well, maybe."

When I later shared the federal crash examiner's findings with my former boss, Dan C. Gainey, he was irate.

The incident became a matter of public record with the federal crash examiner's report. The writer John Grisham captured a very similar incident in describing the loss of an airplane and a life in his book *Gray Mountain*. I sent Grisham an email asking if he would like to write up the story of my airplane loss, but I never received a reply.

Wrapping Up My Business Pursuits

In 1986 I closed the Waseca branch of the Northstar Travel Service. In 1985 Northstar Travel grossed \$1,228,922.24—the Waseca branch grossed \$454,096.38 of that 1.2 million. In March 1988 I signed a deal with Paul Daffinrud, who owned Northwestern Business Travel in Minneapolis, to purchase Northstar Travel Service. The transition finished in August of that year.

As I wrapped up my business pursuits, I sold my real estate assets. On January 3, 1992 we dissolved Northstar, Incorporated after 29 years of successful ventures.

Various articles appeared in the Owatonna People's Press giving a retrospective of my career.

Come Back, Ya Hear?

This is an item of discourse to present to any who have wandered from the traditional values handed down from generations past.

The title is a farewell often given to a departing guest at many places in the southern states. I used it once with what later seemed remarkable results. The occasion was at a gas station in summertime in my community, a red convertible with top down at the fuel pumps, the driver paying her bill as I walked into the building. I immediately recognized the young woman; I had known her in the local 12-step addiction recovery program. She had been doing very well for two years or more but had not been seen at meetings for several months. It didn't take a second look to determine that she was back to her old, destructive habits and also did not want any recognition from me.

But, in a brief moment as she swept toward the door, I said, "Peggy, there's a nice saying down South, 'Come back, ya hear?'" She turned away with a brief expletive, hurried to her car, and left the area with tires squealing and throwing black smoke. "Oh well," I thought; "perhaps I should mind my own business."

A year or so later, at the state recovery program's annual conference in another city, I saw that young woman again. It was at a part of the program designed to recognize and acclaim a man or a woman who had successfully passed that first year milestone in recovery. To my surprise the "one year woman" being recognized, was Peggy. She was a picture of shining happiness, stunningly dressed, wearing a chrysanthemum corsage, and with her hair gracefully styled.

And more surprising, when in the course of recounting her fall and recovery, she related the incident in the gas station. She said that at the time of her last meeting before her fall, she was in the depths of despair thinking that no one cared whether she lived or fell off the face of the earth. It was then that I had said, "Come back, ya hear."

After some reflection on my remark, she went back to her old sponsor and got the encouragement she needed to climb back on the wagon of happy sobriety and aiding others. When she finished her moving story, she was given a standing ovation by the large assembly.

I happened upon her many years after that event at a small meeting in another city. The session had started, and I hadn't expected to see any person I knew. But as I walked to a vacant chair, a lady jumped up and greeted me with a big hug. She told the few people there of her acquaintance with me earlier and of the incident in the gas station. I attempted to minimize my contribution to her happy years in the program saying, "the Lord works in strange ways."

Chapter 9: Articles and Family Photos

Senior Place director Marilyn Flannegan presented Tom Walsh of Owatonna with a runner-up medal after the Senior Spelling Bee regional competition Tuesday. (Press photo by Dave Schwarz)

Red Wing snaps senior streak at SeniorPlace spelling bee

Owatonna spellers miss state 1st time in 5 years

By LAURA COOK
Press New Editor

Owatonna—"Meringue" was the stumper.

However, Barbara Betcher was able to spell the favorite pie topping for the win at Tuesday's regional spelling bee at SeniorPlace.

Owatonn's own Tom Walsh and Ethel Quimby walked away with third and fourth place victories, respectively, after being pushed back by the team from Red Wing, whose spellers Betcher and Emily Flanders will vie at state competition mid-August in Hibbing.

The spelling bee tested competitors with words such as "hosiery" and "xerosis." Word lists are provided through the Scripps Howard National Spelling Bee service.

"It is a challenge," said Marilyn Flanagan, senior citizens director at SeniorPlace.

The challenge is why many seniors become spelling bee participants, she added. Healthy competition brings out the character in some senior citizens who may otherwise be subdued.

"It gives (seniors) a chance to see how they do in competition," Flanagan said.

Walsh hopes more seniors will take advantage of the opportunity to show their skills,

"I'm sure there are a number of good spellers... we just have to encourage them," Walsh said.

"I've always been a good speller," Walsh said. He credits his success to reading books where he often picks up new words.

The spelling bee circuit has been humming for five years, according to Flanagan, who is proud that Owatonna has advanced its regional winners to state competition every year until this year. Owatonna played host to the state competition in 1993.

Seniors are already making plans to brush up on their spelling skills for next year's contest. Scrabble contests and practice spelling rounds are on the agenda, said Flanagan.

"We've already told them to study and prepare for 1996," she said.

Walsh wins Regional Spelling Bee

OWATONNA — Tom Walsh of Owatonna won the Regional Spelling Bee Monday at the Rochester Senior Citizens Center. Walsh participated in the event along with Ethel Quimby and Alice Hines, also of Owatonna.

Walsh captured the senior crown when runner-up Mrs. Virgil Dicke misspelled the word "whinny." After successfully spelling Dieke's miscue, Walsh spelled the word "digitalis" for the Regional Championship.

Walsh will now travel to the State Spelling Bee competition in Mankato July 15 and 16. Walsh, Quimby and Hines are all members of SeniorPlace in Owatonna, which sponsored their enrty in the competition.

Senior citizens take to the lanes

Jeff Cagle/ People's Press

Tom Walsh, 91, steps up and gets ready to bowl the last frame in his final game Monday. He's been bowling for 50 years, saying it provides him good exercise.

by JEFF CAGLE
jcagle@owatonna.com

OWATONNA — With 50 years of bowling—and two hip replacements—under his belt, Tom Walsh showed no signs of slowing down.

Walsh, 91, was able to score a strike and play above his average bowling score of 106 on Monday.

"It's one of the last things I can participate in at my age," he said. "And my wife (of 60 years, Martha Walsh) enjoys it, so I feel like I have to be active with her."

Every Monday, the Walshes participate in the SeniorPlace bowling league at Southpark Lanes. It's a year-round program in which teams bowl three games at a time for eight to nine weeks, including holidays.

The league was organized 20 years ago by Gary Staats, 69, the former owner of the bowling alley and an avid bowler, who enjoys gathering area senior citizens once or twice a week for bowling, coffee and camaraderie.

"The interest is because most of them have been doing it for such a long time," Staats said. "It's one of those things they enjoy."

Numbers can be as low as 24 and as high as 65, Staats said.

Since the beginning of the league, Staats has gone above and beyond, keeping in touch with seniors who have been bowling for a number of years. A lot of seniors who come there, he said, are generally in good shape.

"You lose some people with backs and arms when they leave us," he said.

Walsh said the sport and the league helps him with his recovery and therapy, as well as the exercise it provides. He's not able to swing his hips anymore, which is the reason why he no longer plays golf.

A couple of lanes down, Phyllis Wheeler, 74, suffers from arthritis and take Ibuprofen and Icy Hot cream to help ease the pain. But it hasn't prevented her from bowling some strikes.

"What a show off," one senior joked.

"I haven't done that in a long time," Wheeler gleefully answered

Wheeler especially likes to brag that she began bowling 12 years ago when she was a senior and has been able to get some good scores, including 161 in her second game of the three Monday.

"Like most seniors, one minute we're good and the next minute we're not," she said. "I like it well enough that I'm not going to give it up yet."

Dick Hackerson, 66, just had surgery on one of his hips and isn't able to do as many things as he used to. He also hadn't bowled in 30 years until he began showing up and bowling.

"I never know which hip is going to show up," Hackerson joked.

Along with his running the league, Staats has also paid tribute to 54 bowlers who have died over the years since the league's beginning. Two memorial plaques are located in a trophy case at the side of the bowling alley, giving people an opportunity to see the names and ages of some of the bowling greats in the area.

"I said I'm going to have to be the last one here," Staats said, laughing.

Staats said he also has another bowling program that allows seniors to travel to places like Rochester, Faribault and Waseca once every three weeks prior to the fall season.

Anyone who is interested in joining a bowling league or getting some informations about both leagues is encouraged to call Staats at 451-1477 or SeniorPlace at 444-4280.

Jeff Cagle can be reached at 444-2378.

A Lifelong Admiration Of Flying

Airplanes have always fascinated me. When I was a little kid, I would always look up and stare at a plane flying over my house. Owatonna is right on the flight path of northbound passenger jets heading to the Twin City airport. I always check out the planes flying over Owatonna. When I was a kid living in the Twin Cities, our family would often load up the car and head to the Metropolitan Airport to watch planes landing.

Todd Hale

In his early days of flying in Owatonna, Tom Walsh stands next to the tail of the Jostens Lear Jet. Mr. Gainey chose the 24KT on the tail as an indication of the quality of the product.

An aviation legend

I always enjoyed talking about aviation with my good friend Tom Walsh who many of you know was a corporate pilot for Jostens. He was a legend in local aviation. Tom was one of the founders of the Owatonna Airport along with Glenn Degner, Joe Dulac and Bob Crocker. Tom's aviation career began away from Owatonna. He flew for the New York City Police Department and following that spent two and a half years flying all around the world for Pan American Airways. When the airline ran into financial troubles, Tom left and returned to his home town where he became the corporate pilot for Jostens. He began flying for the company in a single engine Bonanza followed by a Twin Beechcraft. The company then entered the jet age by including a Lear Jet in their plane fleet. Tom flew that in his final years as a corporate pilot.

Tom eventually started his area own charter service, flying his own plane. Another aviation thrill for me was when he invited me to fly to the Twin Cities with him and we landed at the Metropolitan Airport. I was fascinated by the radio transmissions and the other airliner traffic around us and Tom amazed me when he honed in on the signal of KRFO and brought us right back to Owatonna. It was a sad day for Tom when his plane caught fire in Mankato and was destroyed. All in all, his aviation career lasted over 30 years. "The only injury I had in all that time was when the door of the Lear Jet closed on me and I suffered a cut on my head." Tom said. Tom continued to serve the Airport Commission for many years.

Frances Collins Walsh and Thomas J. Walsh, date unknown.

Tom and Martha Walsh

Family of Tom and Martha Walsh

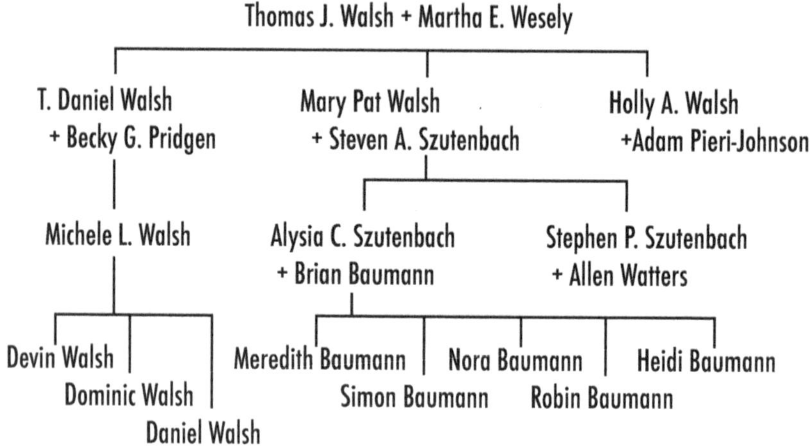

Tom and Martha with their children, Daniel Walsh, Holly Walsh and Mary Pat (Walsh) Szutenbach.

Mary Pat, Daniel and Holly, with Tom.

Holly, Daniel and Mary Pat, with Tom.

Back row: Steven and Mary Pat Szutenbach, Alysia and Brian Baumann, Michele Walsh, Dan Walsh, Holly Walsh, and Adam Pieri-Johnson. Front row: Simon, Nora, Robin, and Meredith Baumann, and Tom Walsh

Dan's daughter Michele with her 3 sons.
From left: Dominic, Michele holding Dan, and Devin.

Alysia and Brian Baumann with their children,
Robin (front), Simon and Nora (middle),
Heidi (held by Alysia) and Meredith.

www.ingramcontent.com/pod-product-compliance
Lightning Source LLC
LaVergne TN
LVHW091632100826
845152LV00001B/16